EARLY ITALIAN
ART

Author: Joseph Archer Crowe and Giovanni Battista Cavalcaselle Anna Jameson

Layout:
Baseline Co. Ltd,
District 3, Ho Chi Minh City
Vietnam

ISBN: 978-1-68325-920-6

Printed in

Joseph Archer Crowe & Giovanni Battista Cavalcaselle Anna Jameson

EARLY ITALIAN ART

From Giotto to the Renaissance dawn

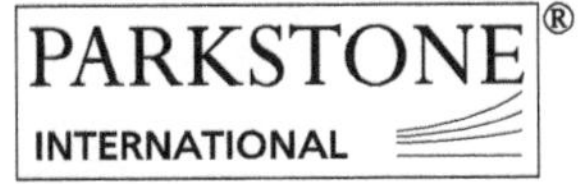

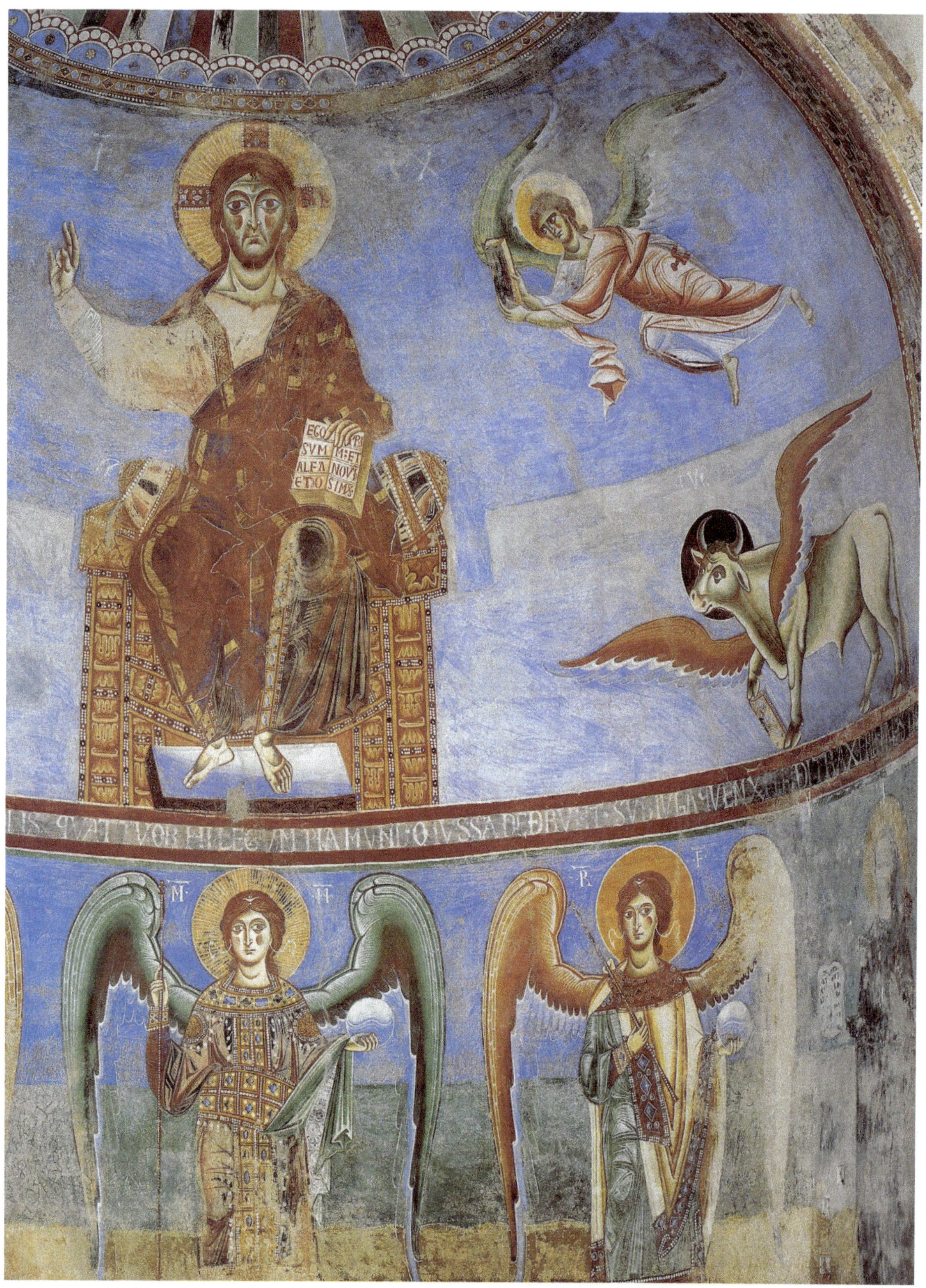

CONTENTS

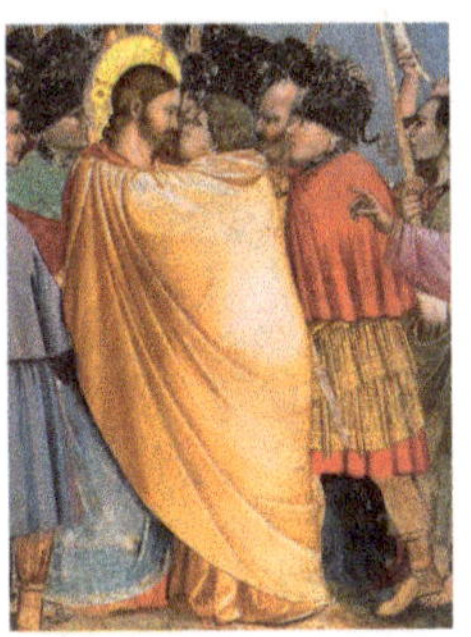

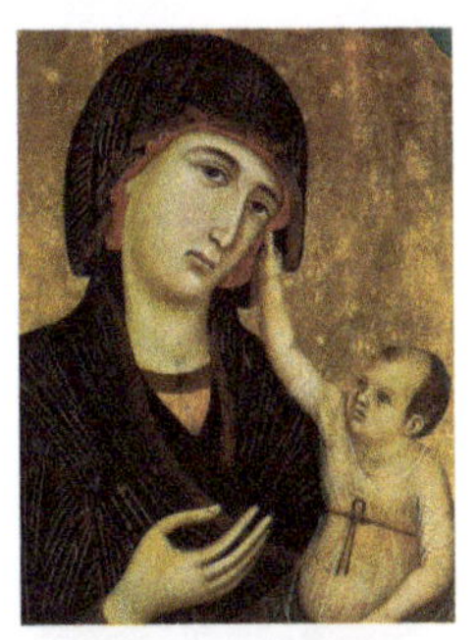

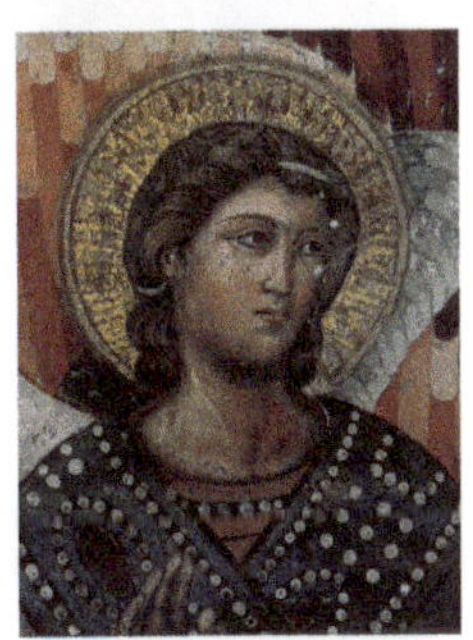

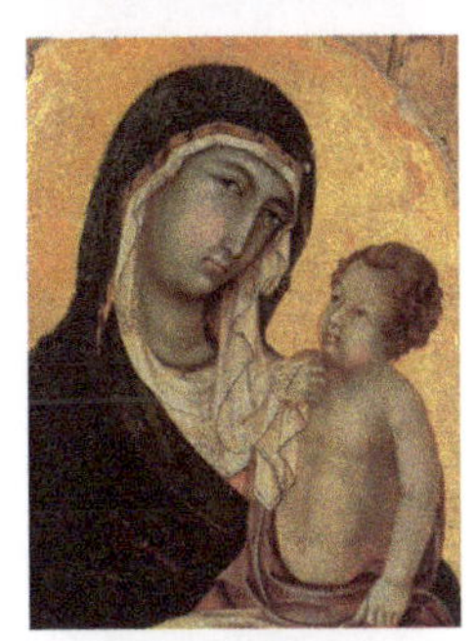

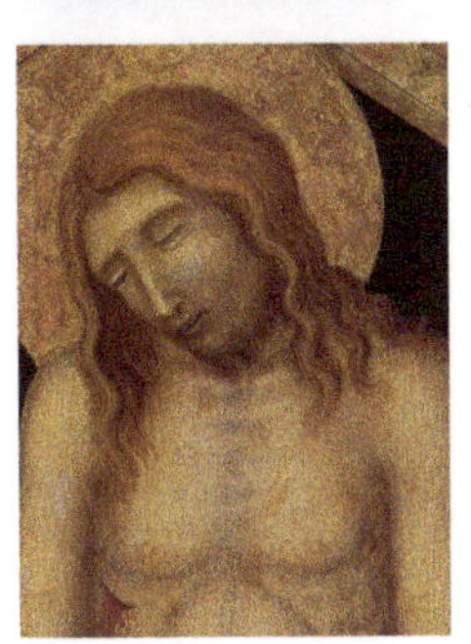

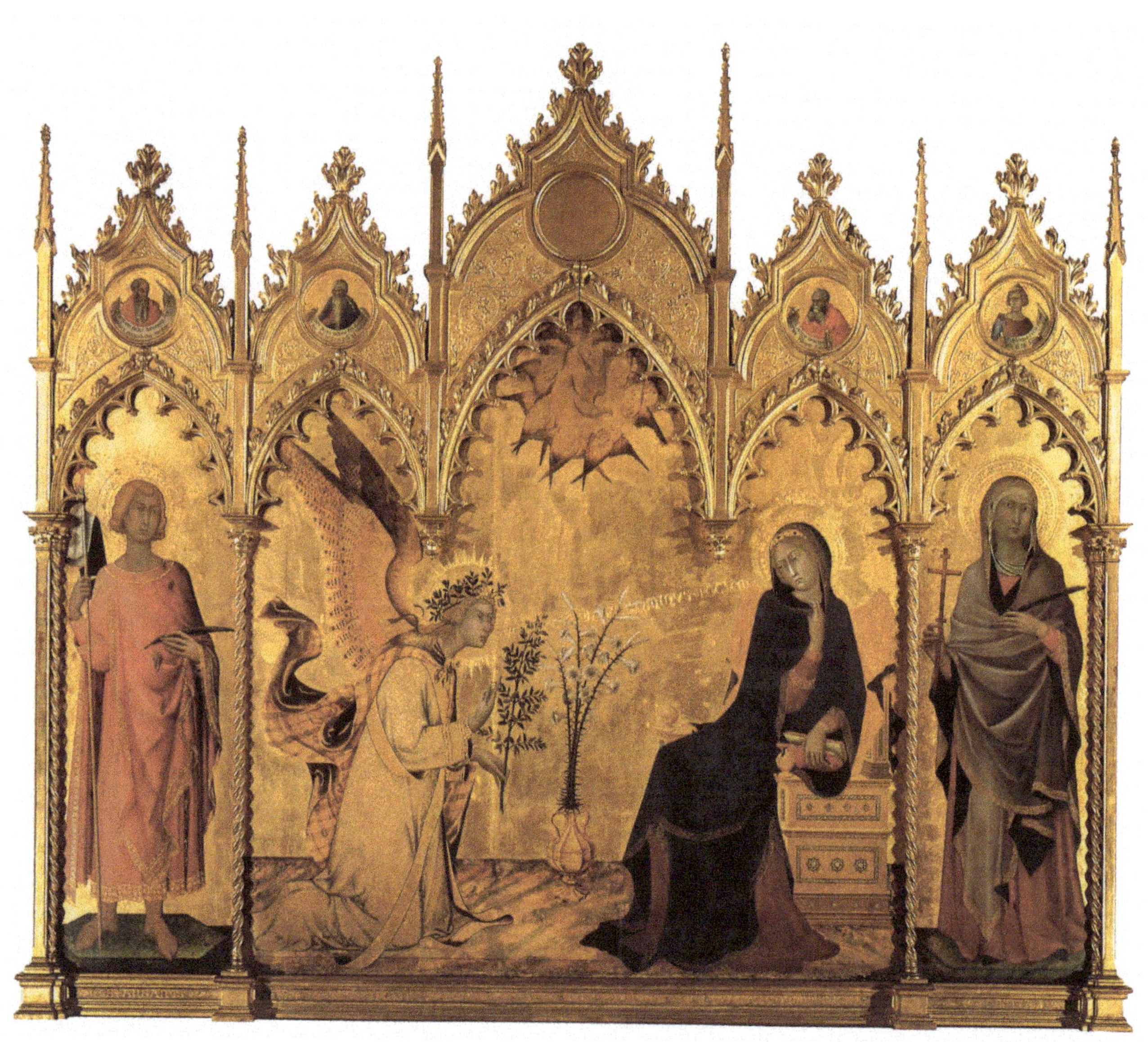

INTRODUCTION

The progress made in painting was predominantly achieved by carrying out the principles of Giotto in expression and in imitation. Taddeo Gaddi and Simone excelled in the first; the imitation of form and of natural objects was evolved by Stefano Fiorentino, so much so that he was styled by his contemporaries as "*Il Scimia della Natura*", or "the Ape of Nature". Giottino, the son of Stefano, and others, improved in color, in softness of execution, and in the means and technology of the art; but oil painting was not yet invented, and linear perspective was unknown. Engraving on copper, cutting in wood, and printing, were the inventions of the next century. Portraits were seldom painted, and were only ever of very distinguished persons, introduced into larger compositions. The imitation of natural scenery, that is, landscape painting, as a branch of art now so familiar a source of pleasure, was as yet unthought-of. When landscape was introduced into pictures as a background or accessory, it was merely to indicate the scene of the story: a rock represented a desert; some laconic trees, much like upside-down brooms, indicated a wood; a bluish space, sometimes with fishes in it, signified, rather than represented, a river or a sea. Yet in the midst of this simplicity, this imperfect execution and limited range of power, how exquisitely beautiful are some of the remains of this early time! The simple, genuine grace and lofty, earnest feeling that marks these works have provided modern painters with examples of emotive excellence to be understood and techniques which the great Raphael himself did not disdain to study and even copy.

The purpose to which painting was applied during this embryonic period was almost wholly of a religious character. No sooner was a church erected than the walls were covered with representations of sacred subjects, either from scriptural history or the legends of saints. Devout individuals or families built and consecrated chapels; and then, at a great cost, employed painters either to decorate the walls or to paint pictures for the altars. The Madonna and Child

▲ **Christ in Majesty**, c. 1072-1087.
Fresco.
Basilica of Sant'Angelo in Formis, Capua.

◀ **Simone Martini** and **Lippo Memmi**,
Altarpiece of The Annunciation, 1333.
Tempera on wood, 184 x 210 cm.
Galleria degli Uffizi, Florence.

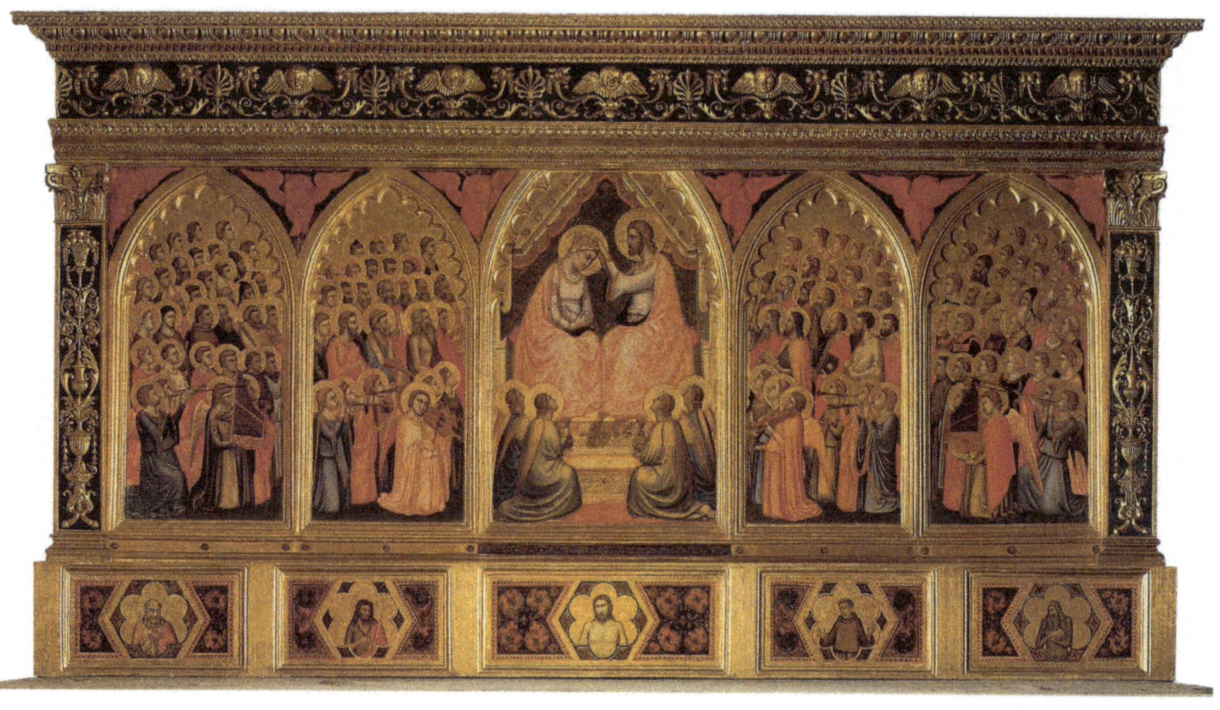

or the Crucifixion of Christ were the favorite subjects; the donor of the picture or founder of the chapel was often represented on his knees in a corner of the picture, and sometimes (as a more obvious expression of humility) in a most diminutive size, out of all proportion to the other figures. Where the object was to commemorate the dead, or to express both the grief and devotion of the survivors, the subject was generally a "Deposition from the Cross" — that is, Christ taken down from the cross and lying in the arms of his afflicted mother. The

doors of the sacristies, and of the presses in which the priests' vestments were kept, were often covered with small pictures of scriptural subjects, as were the chests in which the utensils for the Holy Sacrament were deposited. Almost all the small moveable pictures of the fourteenth and fifteenth centuries that have come down to us are either the borders or small compartments cut out from the broken-up altarpieces of chapels and oratories, or from the panels of doors, the covers of chests, or other pieces of ecclesiastical furniture.

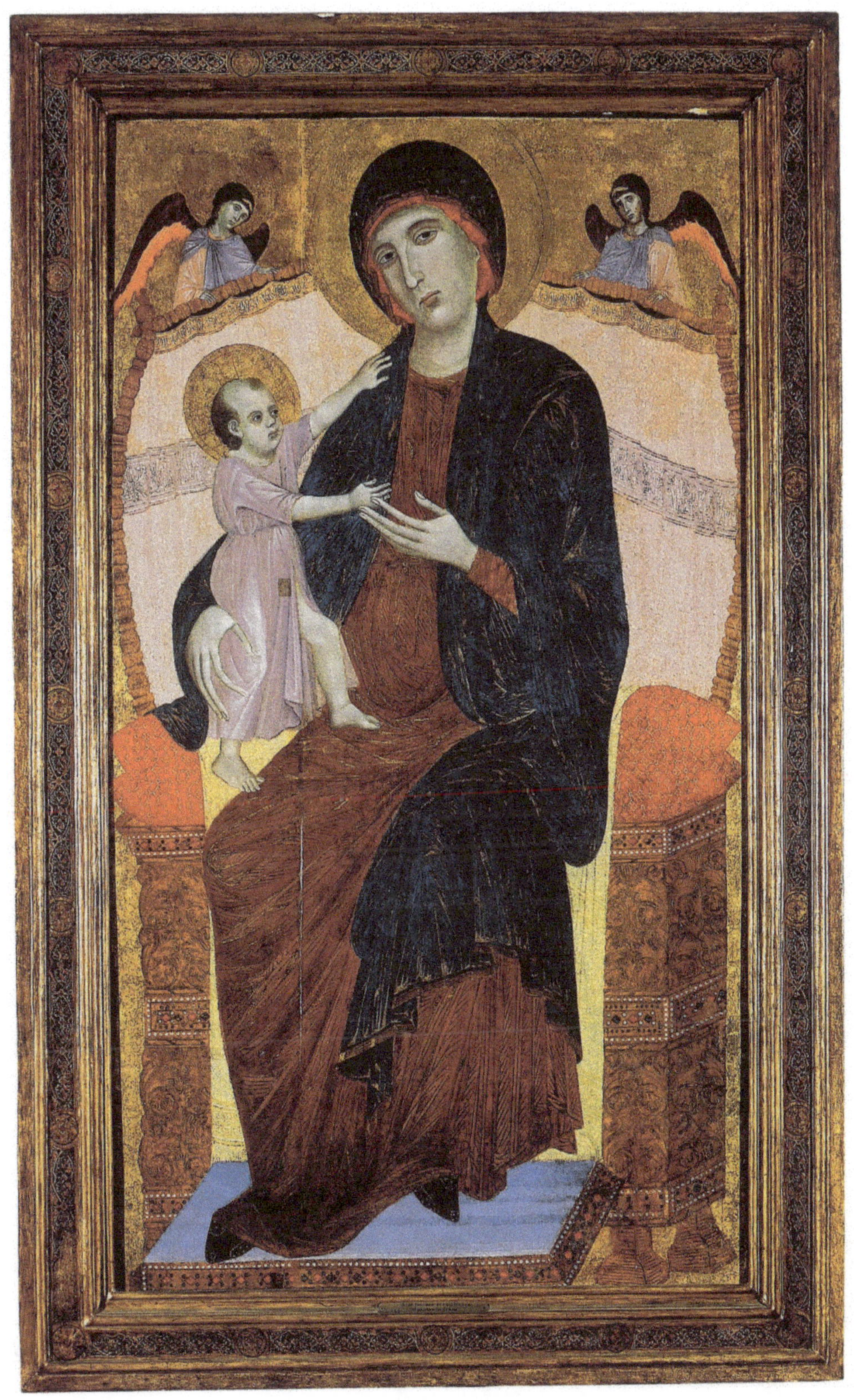

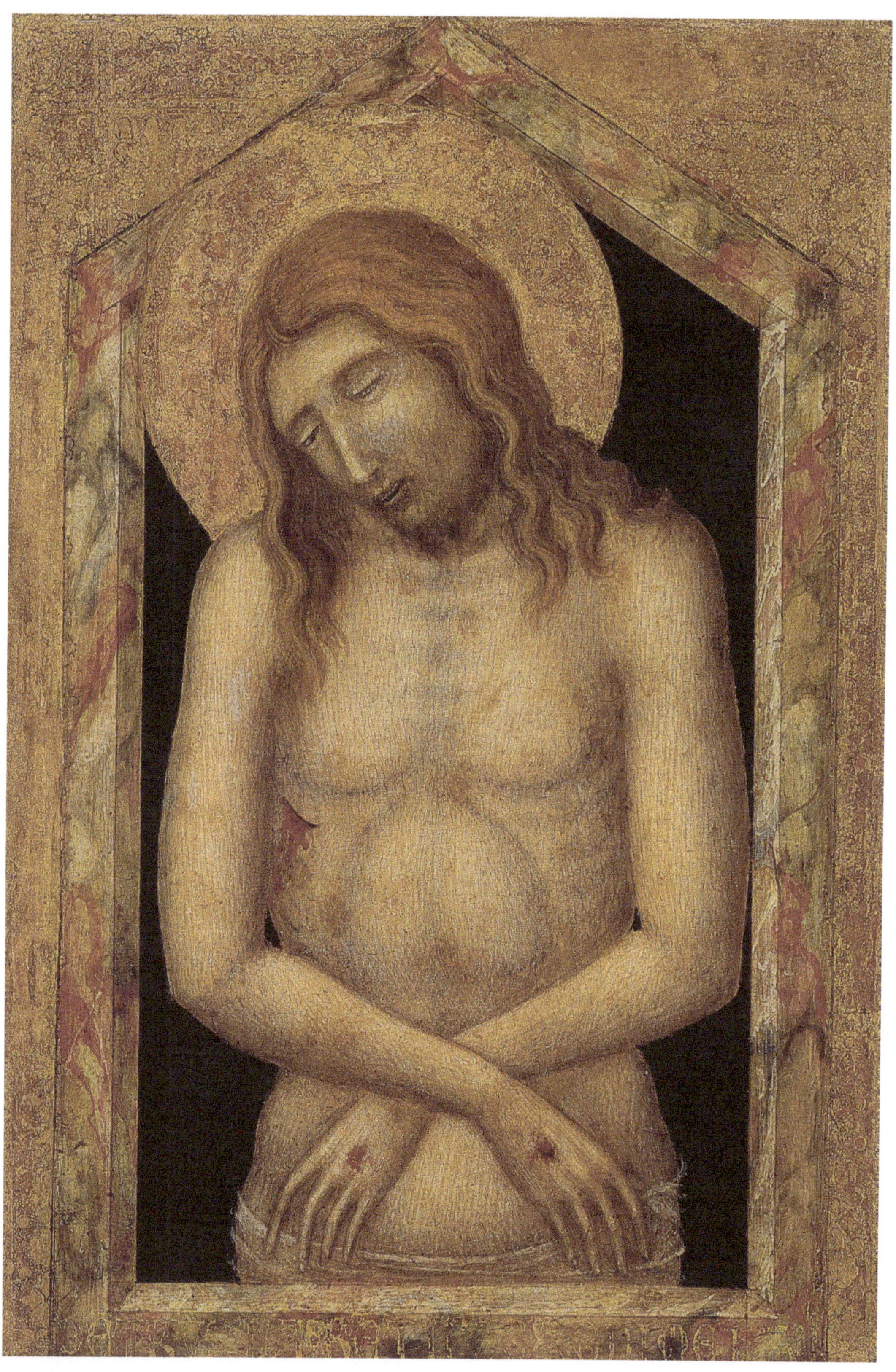

EARLY CHRISTIANITY AND ART

The early Christians confounded in their horror of heathen idolatry all imitative art and artists; they regarded with decided hostility all images and those who created them as bound to the service of Satan and heathenism. Hence, all visible representations of sacred personages and actions were therefore confined to mystic emblems. Thus, crosses signified redemption; fish, baptism; ships represented the church; serpents, sin or the spirit of evil. When, in the fourth century, the struggle between paganism and Christianity ended in the triumph and dominance of the latter and artistic activity was revived, it was, if not in a new form, in a new spirit through which the old forms were to be gradually molded and modified.

The Christians found the shell of ancient art remaining; traditional handicraft still existed. Certain models of figure and drapery handed down from antiquity, though degenerated and distorted, remained in use, and were applied to illustrate, by direct or symbolic representations the tenets of a purer faith. From the beginning, the figures selected to typify redemption were those of Christ

◀ **Pietro Lorenzetti,**
Christ of Compassion (facing right), between 1340-1345.
Lindenau-Museum, Altenburg.

and the Virgin, first separately and then conjointly as the 'Mother and Infant'.

The earliest monuments of Christian art are to be found, nearly effaced, on the walls and ceilings of the catacombs at Rome, to which the early persecuted martyrs of the faith had fled for refuge. The first recorded representation of Christ is in the character of the 'Good Shepherd', and the attributes of Orpheus and Apollo were borrowed to express the character of he who "redeemed souls from hell", and "gathered his people like sheep". In the cemetery of St. Calixtus in Rome, the most ancient depiction was discovered: a head of Christ. The figure is colossal; the face a long oval; the countenance mild, grave, melancholy; the long hair parted on the brow and falling in two masses on either shoulder; the beard not thick, but short and divided. Here then, obviously imitated from some traditional description, we have the first emergence of the type, the generic character since adhered to in the representations of Christ.

A controversy arose afterwards in the early Christian Church which had a determinately significant influence on art as it subsequently developed. One party, with St. Cyril at its head, maintained that the form of Christ, having been described by the prophet as without any outward comeliness, ought to be represented as utterly hideous and repulsive in painting. Fortunately, as the future success of the faith would prove, the most eloquent and influential among the fathers of the Church, St. Jerome, St. Augustine, St. Ambrose, and St. Bernard, took up the opposing side of the argument. The pope, Adrian I, also threw his infallibility into the scale, and from the eighth century we find it decided, and later confirmed by a papal bull, that Christ should be represented with all the attributes of divine beauty which art in its then unrefined state could lend him.

Since that time the accepted and traditional type for the representation of Christ has been strictly attended to — a tall, slender figure with a long oval face; broad, serene, elevated brows; a mild, melancholy, and majestic countenance; the hair parted in the front, and flowing down on each side; and a parted beard. The resemblance to his mother — his only earthly parent — was strongly insisted upon by the early ecclesiastical writers and attended to by the earliest painters, which has given something peculiarly refined and even feminine to the most ancient artistic representations of Christ.

The oldest representations of the Virgin Mary now remaining are the sculptures on ancient Christian sarcophagi of about the third and fourth centuries, and a mosaic in the chapel of San Venanzio at Liome, referred to by antiquarians, emanating from the seventh century. Here she is represented as a colossal figure, draped majestically, standing with outspread arms and her eyes raised to heaven; then, after the seventh century succeeding her image in her maternal character: seated on a throne with the infant Christ in her arms. We must bear in mind, once and for all, that from the earliest ages of Christianity, the Virgin mother of Christ has been selected as the allegorical embodiment of religion in the abstract sense; to this, her symbolic character must be lended those representations of later times, in which she appears trampling on the dragon, folding her votaries within the skirts of her ample robe, interceding for sinners, and crowned between heaven and earth by the Father and the Son.

In the same manner, traditional heads of St. Peter and St. Paul, roughly sketched, later became the groundwork of the highest dignity and beauty, still retaining that peculiarity of form and character which time and custom had consecrated in the eyes of the devout.

Besides the representations of Christ and the Virgin, some of the characters and incidents of the Old Testament were selected as subjects of art, generally with reference to corresponding characters and incidents in the Gospel. Thus, St. Augustine, in the latter half of the fourth century, tells us that "Abraham offering up his son Isaac"

Duccio di Buoninsegna, ▶
Crevole Madonna, c. 1280.
Tempera on wood.
Museo dell'Opera del Duomo, Siena.

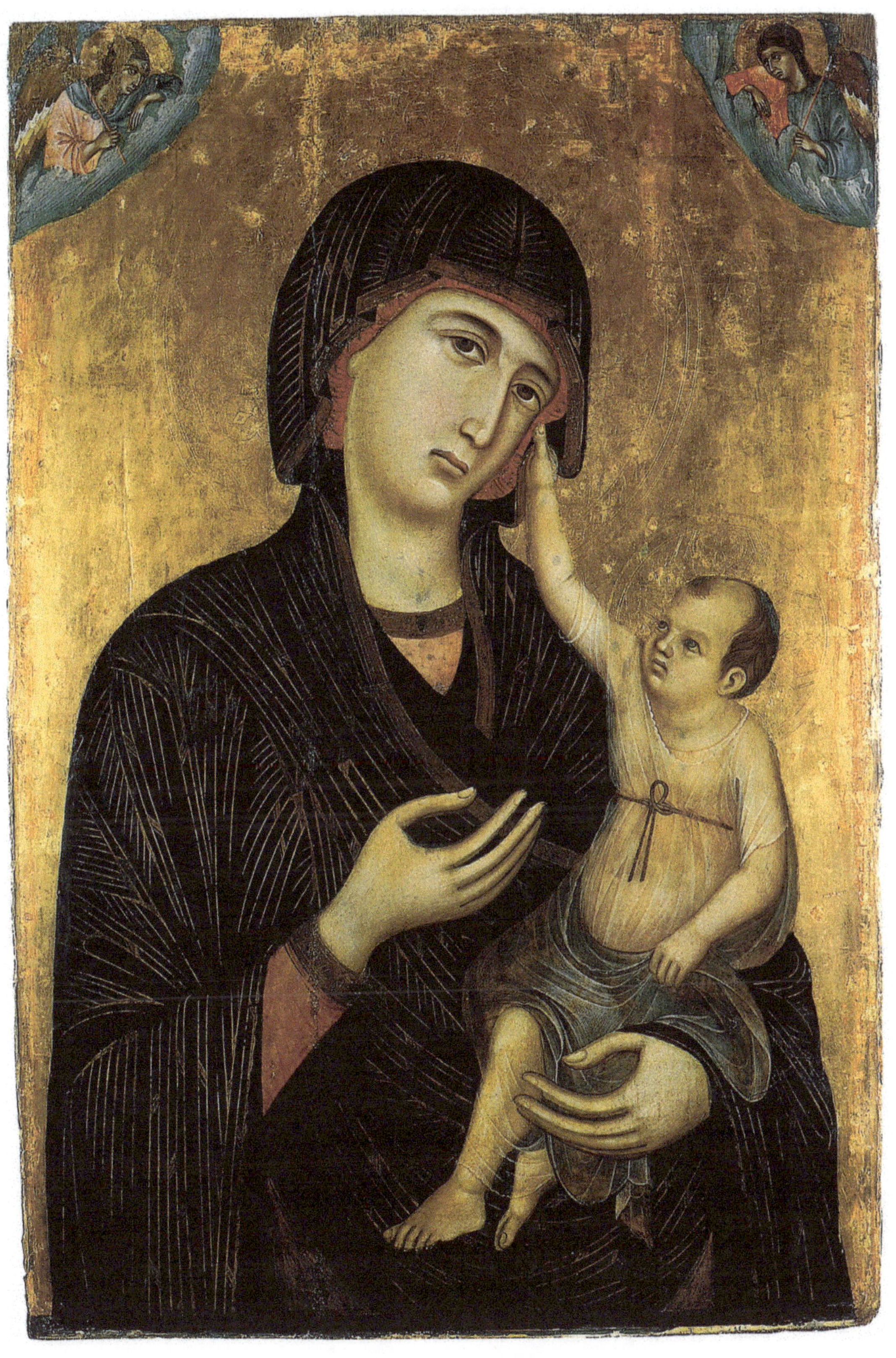

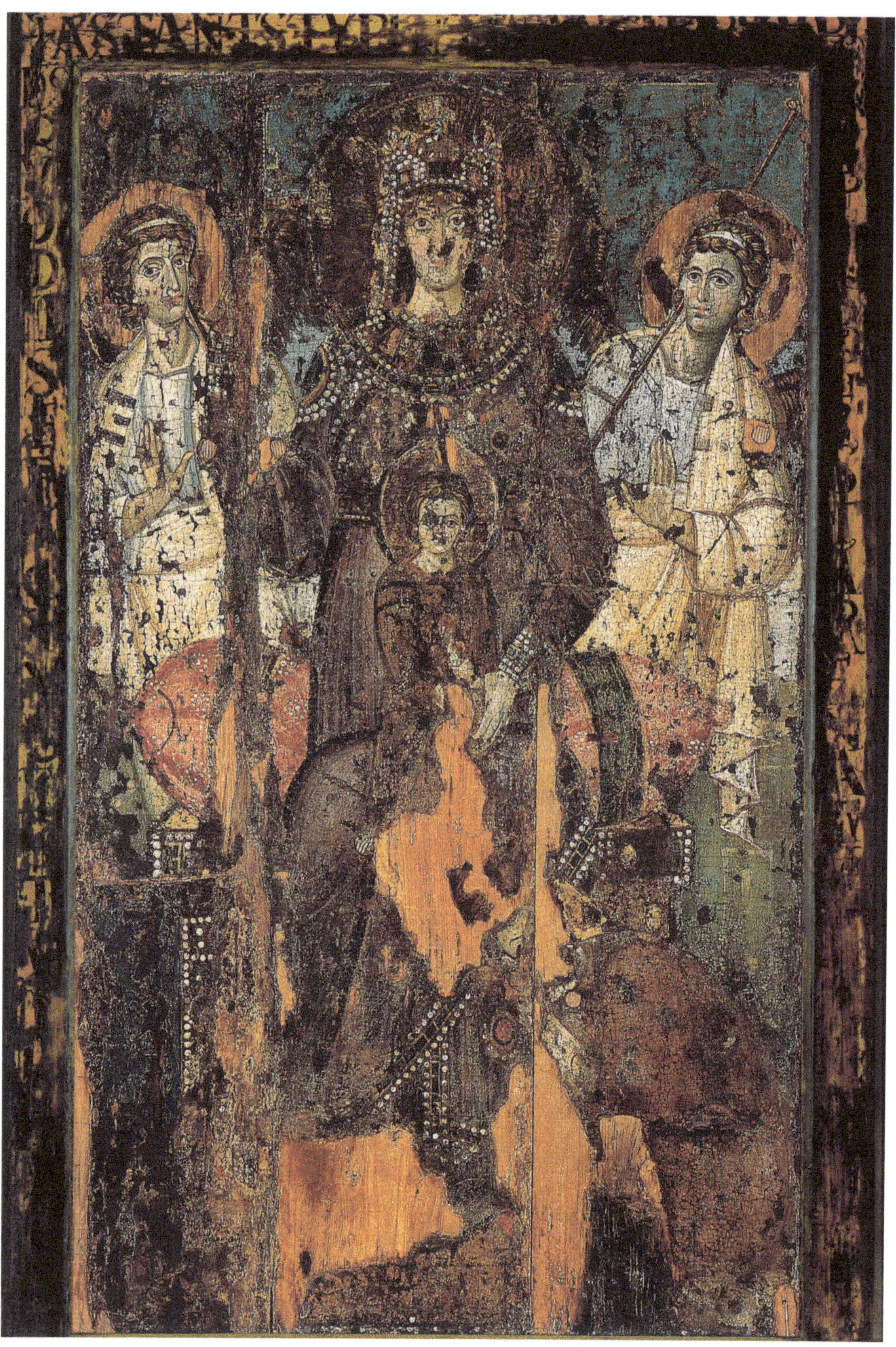

was then a common subject, typical, of course, of the sacrifice of the Son of God; "Moses striking the rock," the Gospel or the water of life; the vine or grapes expressed the sacrament of the Eucharist; Jonah swallowed by the whale and then disgorged signified death and resurrection; Daniel in the lions' den signified redemption. This system of corresponding subjects, of type and antitype, was later, as we shall see, taken much further.

In the seventh century, painting, as it existed in Europe, may be divided into two great schools or styles — the Western, or Roman, of which the central point was Rome, and which was distinguished, amid great harshness of execution, by a certain dignity of expression and solemnity of feeling; and the Eastern, or Byzantine school, which was headquartered in Constantinople, and which was distinguished by greater mechanical skill by adherence to the old classical forms, by the use of gilding, and by the mean, vapid, spiritless conception of motive and character.

From the fifth to the ninth century, the most important and interesting remains of pictorial art are the mosaics in the churches and the miniature

◀ **The Mother of God between two angels**, *Madonna Della Clemenza*, c. 700. Icon with encaustic, 164 cm. Santa Maria in Trastevere, Rome.

▼ **Master of St. Cecilia**, *St. Cecilia Surrounded by Eight Episodes of Her Life*, 1304 or later. Tempera on wood, 85 x 181 cm. Galleria degli Uffizi, Florence.

paintings with which the Bible and Gospel manuscripts were decorated.

But during the tenth and eleventh centuries, Italy fell into a state of complete barbarism and confusion, which almost extinguished the practice of art in any shape; of this period only a few works remain. In the Byzantine Empire, painting still survived; it became, indeed, more and more conventional, but the technical methods were kept up. And so it happened when, in 1204, Constantinople was taken by the Crusaders and the intercourse between the east and west of Europe was resumed that several Byzantine painters passed into Italy and Germany where they were employed to decorate churches, and taught the practice of their art, their manner of penciling, mixing and using colors, and gilding ornaments to students who chose to learn them. They brought over the Byzantine types of form and color, the long lean limbs of the saints, the dark-visaged Madonnas, and the blood-streaming crucifixes; these patterns were followed more or less imitatively by the native Italian painters who studied under them.

Specimens of this early art remain, and in later times have been diligently sought and collected into museums as curiosities, illustrating the history and progress of art. As such, they are interesting in the highest degree, but it must be confessed that otherwise they are not conventionally attractive. There are some very valuable examples in the Royal Collection of Britain. There is also one in the National Icon Collection of the British Museum, a little Cretan picture of the famous Apothecary

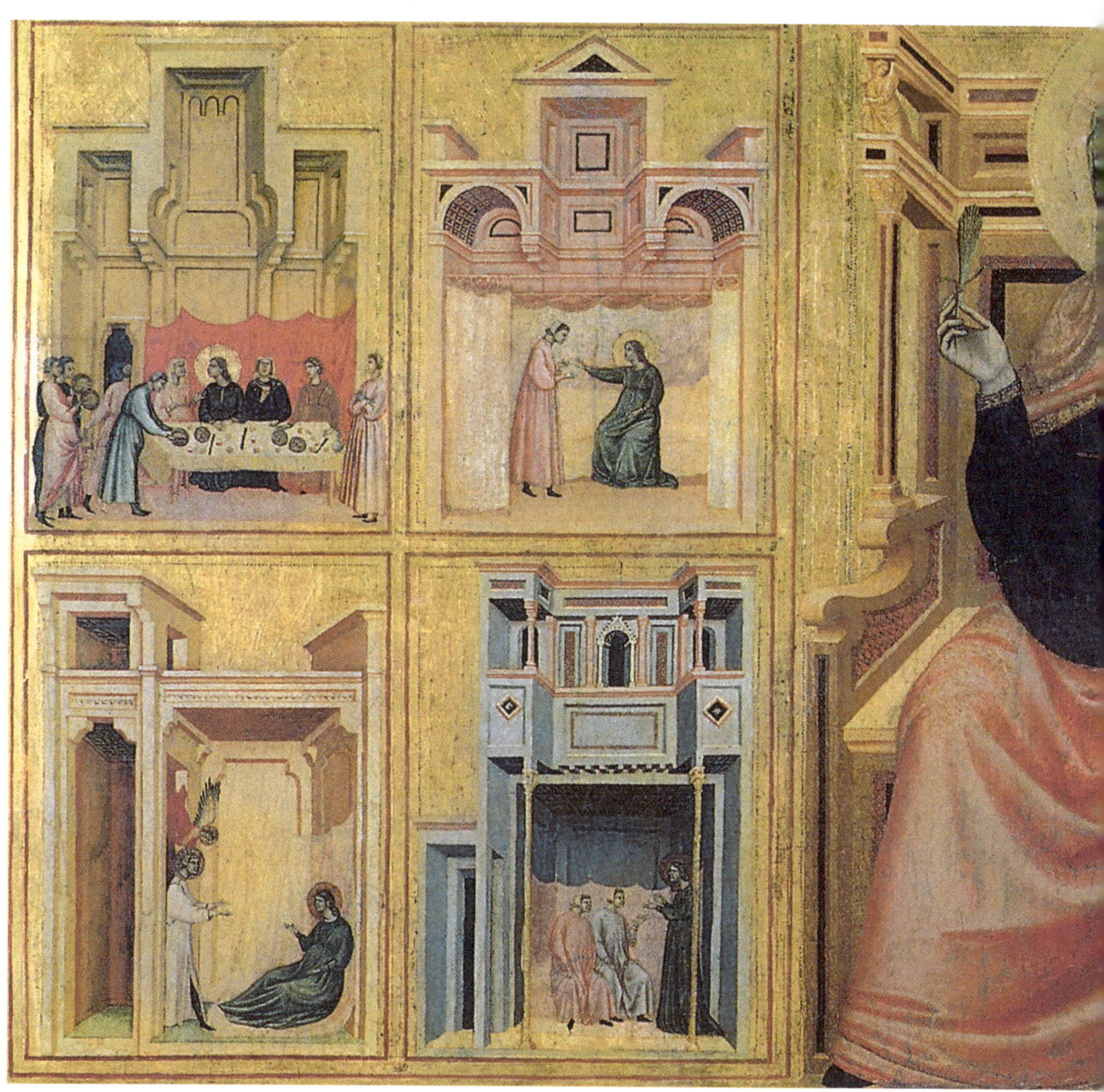

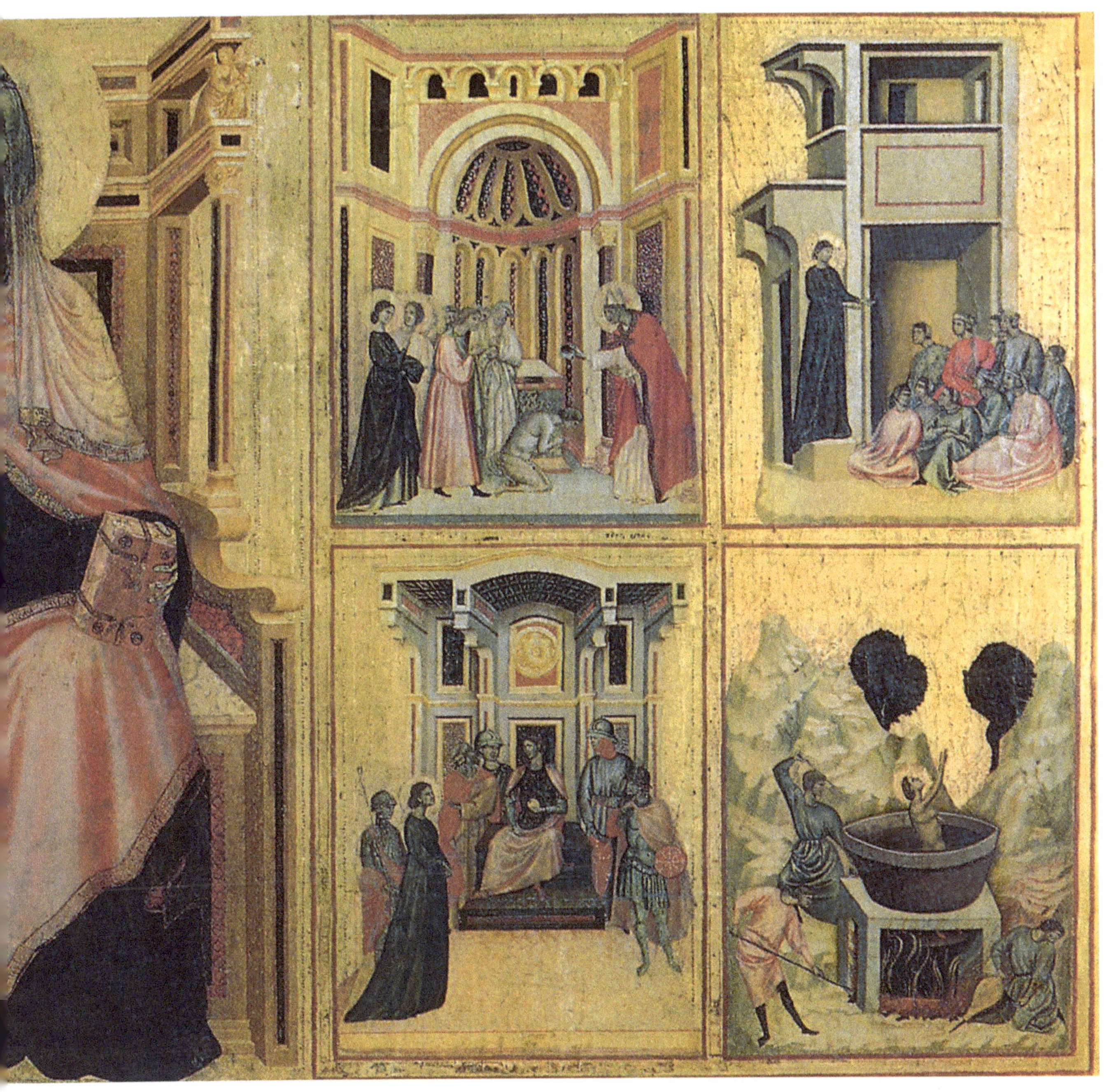

Saints, Cosmo and Damian, painted by a certain Emanuel Tzanes, in the seventeenth century. In the "Gemäldegalerie in Berlin", the "Galleria degli Uffizi" in Florence, and in the Louvre, a few Greek pictures are preserved as curiosities. The subject is generally the Madonna and Child enthroned, sometimes alone, sometimes with angels or saints ranged on each side. The characteristics in all cases are the same: the figures are stiff with long and meager extremities, the features are hard and expressionless, and the eyes are long and narrow.

The head of the Virgin is generally declined to the left: the infant Christ is clothed and sometimes crowned; two fingers of his right hand are extended in an act of benediction; the left hand holding a globe, a scroll, or a book. With regard to the execution, the ornaments of the throne and borders of the draperies, and frequently the background, are elaborately gilded. The local colors are generally vivid and there is little or no relief; the handling is streaky and the flesh tints are blackish or greenish. At this time, and for two hundred years afterwards, pictures were painted either in fresco, an art never totally lost, or on panels of seasoned wood, the colors mixed with water and thickened with egg white or the juice of the young shoots of the fig tree. This last method was styled by the Italians *a colla* or *tempera*; by the French, *en détrempe*; and in English, in distemper. It is in these manners that all movable pictures were executed prior to 1440.

As it is not the purpose of this book to trace the gradual progress of early art, but rather to give some account of the early artists, and, as we know, nothing of those who lived in the first half of the thirteenth century except a name and date inscribed on a picture, there is no use dwelling upon them, but only revert to the fact that before the birth of Cimabue (1200-1240) there existed schools of painting in Siena and Pisa, not only under Greek but also Italian instruction. The former city produced Guido, whose *Madonna and Child*, with life-sized figures, signed and dated 1221, and preserved in the Palazzo Pubblica of Siena. It is engraved in Rosini's *Storia della Pittura*, on the same page with a *Madonna* by Cimabue, to which it appears superior in drawing, attitude, expression, and drapery. Pisa produced Giunta da Pisa around the same time, of whom there remain works with the date 1236, one of these is a *Crucifixion*, engraved in Ottley's *Italian School of Design*, and on a smaller scale in Rosini's *Storia della Pittura*, in which the expression of grief in the hovering angels, who are wringing their hands and weeping, is very emotive and striking. Undoubtedly, though, the greatest man of that time, who gave an ingenutive impulse to modern art, was a sculptor, Nicola Pisano, whose works date from about 1220 to 1270. Further, it appears that even in Florence a native painter, a certain Maestro Bartolomeo, lived and was employed in 1236. Thus, Cimabue's often-quoted title as 'father of modern painting' cannot be justified, even in his own city of Florence.

Crucifixion, mid 8th century. ▶
Fresco, 140 x 155 cm.
Teodoto Chapel, Santa Maria Antiqua, Rome.

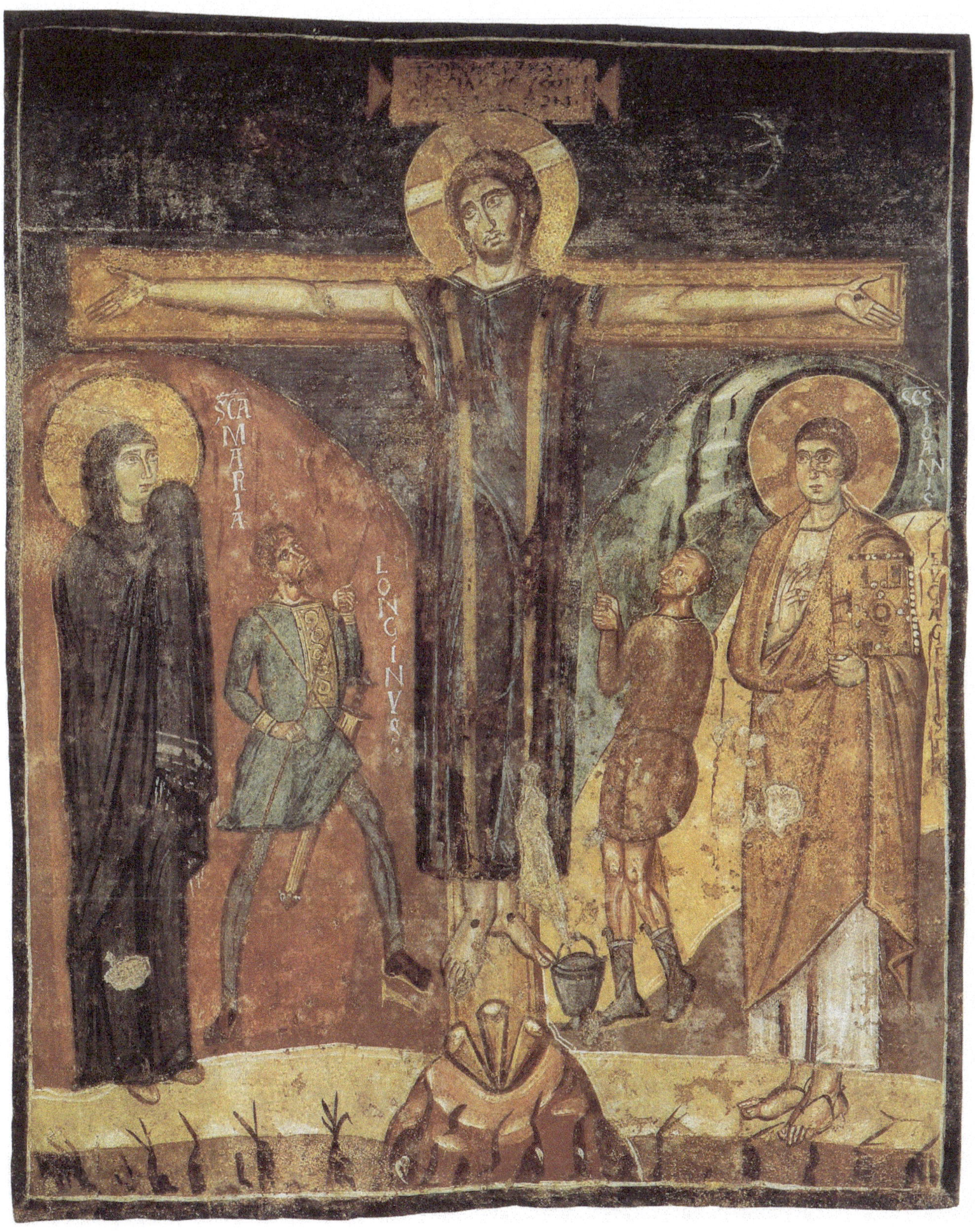
SCA
MARIA
LONGINVS
SCS
IOANNIS
EVANGELISTA

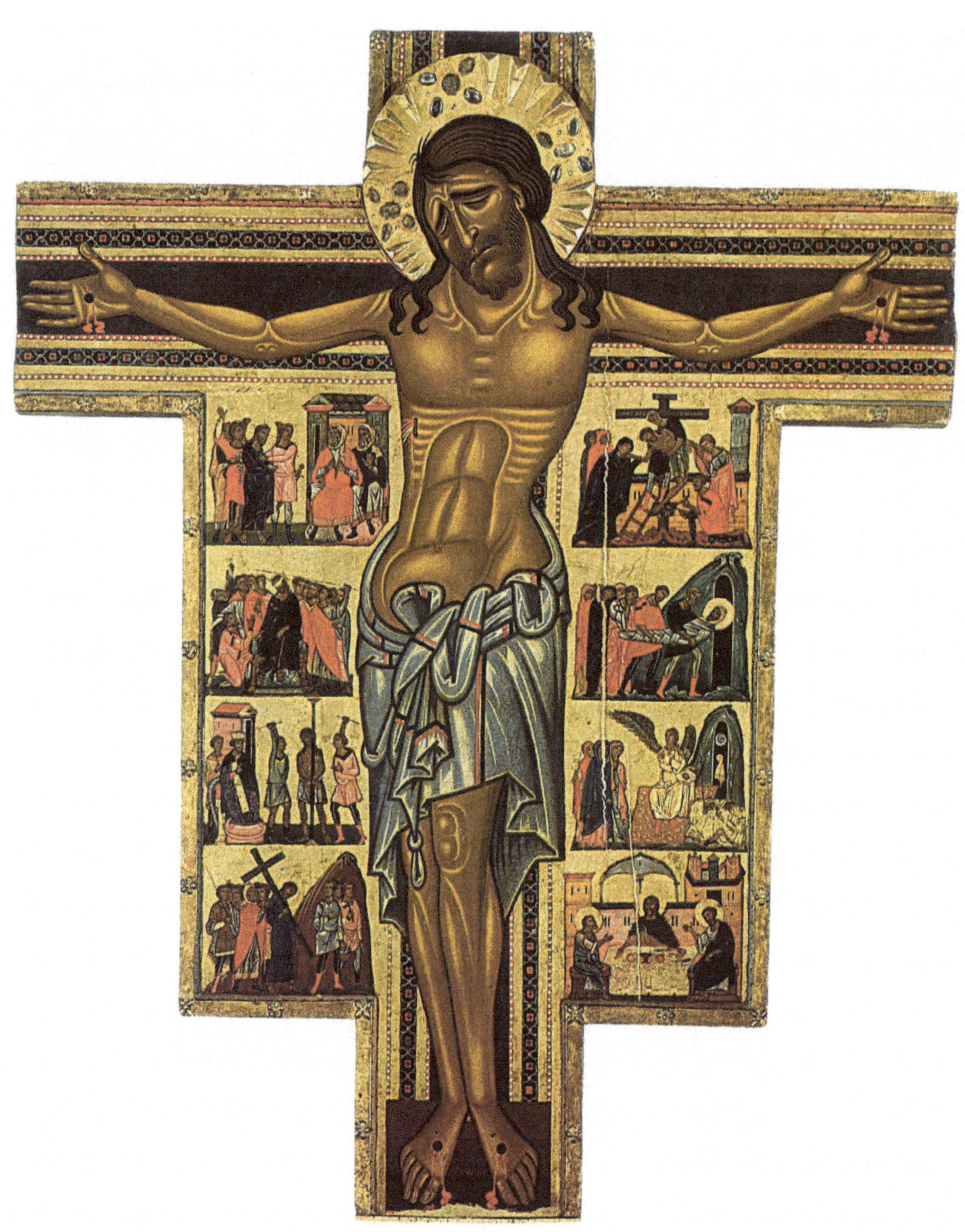

▲ **Master of the Crucifixion**, *Crucifixion and Eight Episodes of the Passion of the Christ*,
end of the 12th century to the beginning of the 13th.
Tempera on wood, 250 x 200 cm. Galleria degli Uffizi, Florence.

THE EARLY ITALIAN PAINTERS

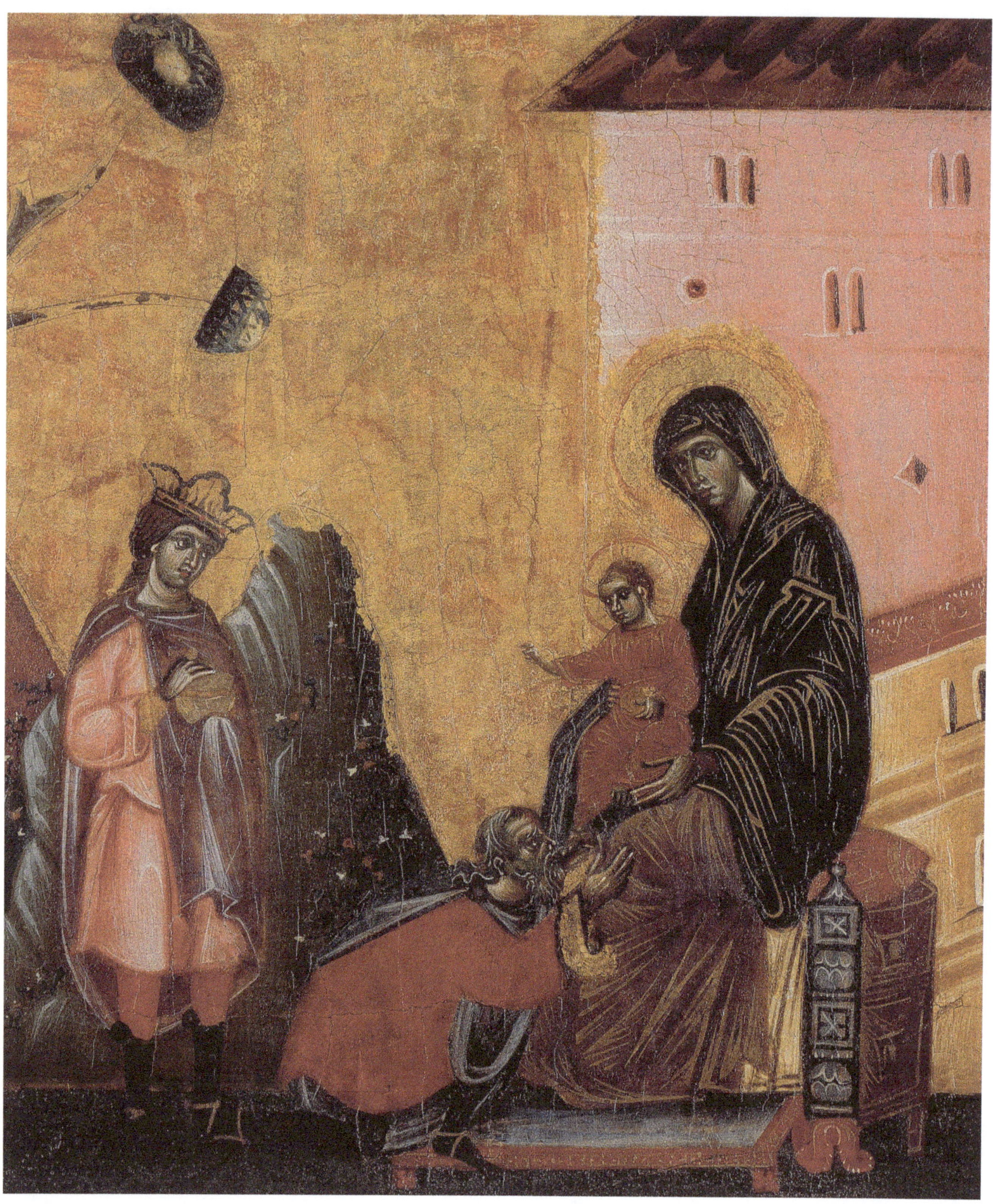

GUIDO DA SIENA

13th century

The name of this Italian painter is of considerable interest in the history of art, on the ground that, if certain assumptions regarding him could be accepted as true, he would be entitled to share with Cimabue, or rather indeed to supersede him in the honour of having given the first onward impulse to the art of painting. The case stands thus. In the church of S. Domenico in Siena is a large painting of the *Virgin and Child Enthroned*, with six angels above, and in the Benedictine convent of the same city is a triangular pinnacle, once a portion of the same composition, representing the Saviour in benediction, with two angels; the entire work was originally a triptych, but is not so now. The principal section of this picture has a rhymed Latin inscription, giving the painter's name as Gu...o de Senis, with the date of 1221; the genuineness of the inscription is not, however, free from doubt, and especially it is maintained

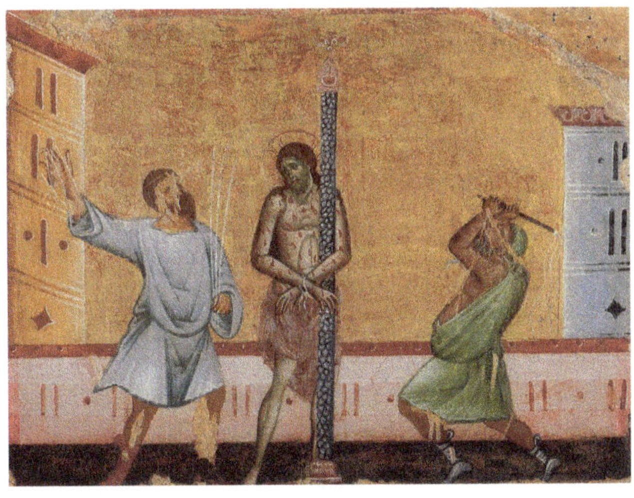

that the date really reads 1281. In the great treatment of the picture there is nothing to distinguish it particularly from other work of the same early period, but the heads of the Virgin and Child are indisputably very superior, in natural character and graceful dignity to anything to be found anterior to Cimabue.

Beyond this, little is known of Guido da Siena. There is in the Academy of Siena a picture assigned to him, a half-figure of the *Virgin and Child*, with two angels, probably dating between 1250 and 1300; also in the church of S. Bernardino in the same city a Madonna dated 1262.

◀ **Guido da Siena,**
The Adoration of the Magi (detail), c. 1270-1280.
Lindenau-Museum, Altenburg.

▲ **Guido da Siena,**
The Flagellation, c. 1270-1280.
Lindenau-Museum, Altenburg.

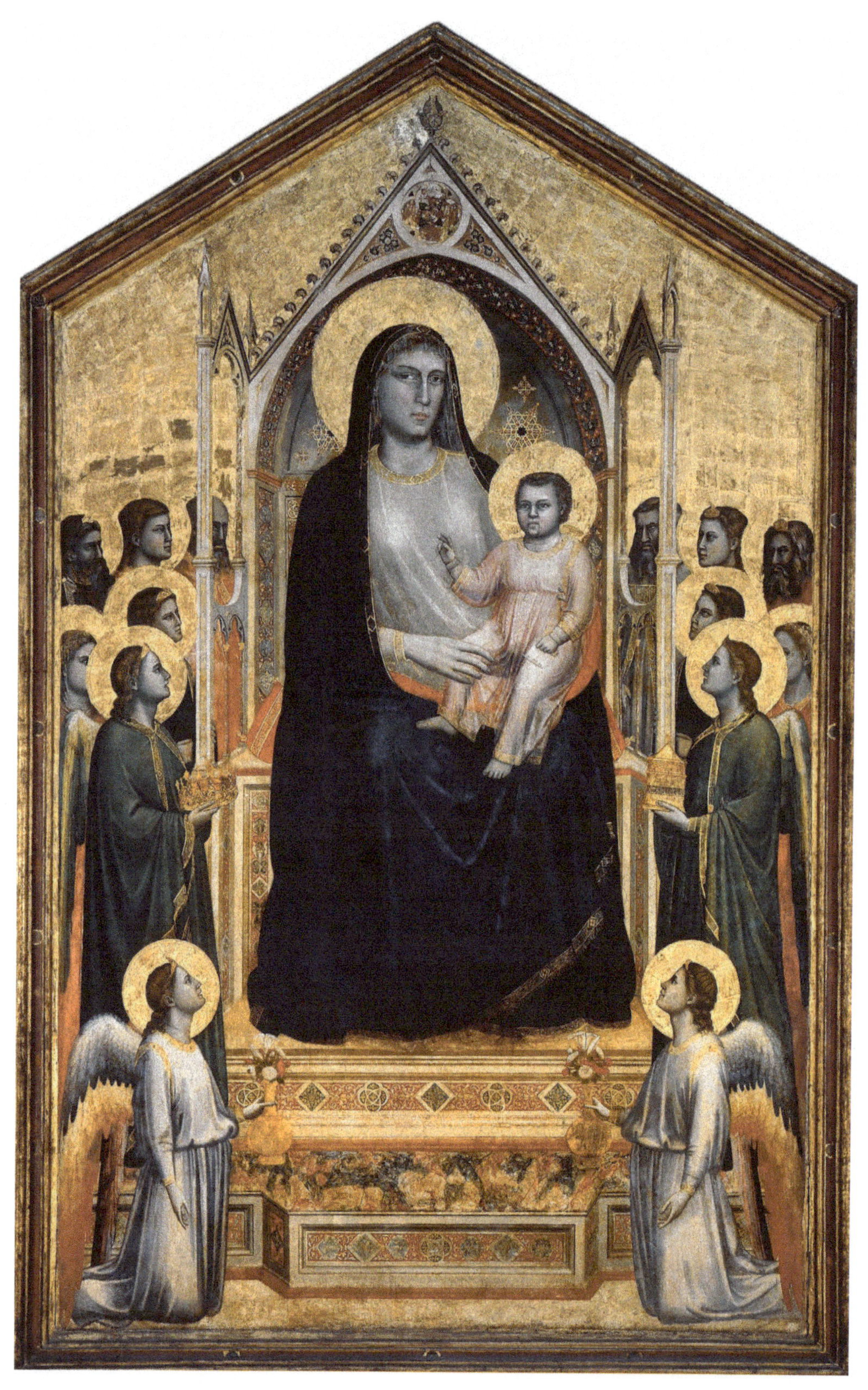

GIOVANNI CIMABUE

1240-1302

Giovanni Cimabue was born in Florence of a respectable family, which seems to have borne the name of Gualtieri, as well as that of Cimabue (Bullhead). He took to the arts of design by natural inclination and sought the society of men of learning and accomplishment. He was the most advanced master of his time, and, by his own works, and the training he imparted to his mighty pupil Giotto, he left the art far more formed and more capable of growth than he found it.

The undoubted admiration of his contemporaries would alone demonstrate the conspicuous position which Cimabue held and deserved to hold. For the chapel of the Rucellai in S. Maria Novella he painted in tempera a colossal *Madonna and Child with Angels*, the largest altarpiece produced up to that date, before its removal from the studio it was visited with admiration by Charles of Anjou, with a host of eminent men and gentle ladies, and it was carried to the church in a festive procession of the people and trumpeters. This celebrated picture is one of the great landmarks of sacred art.

In a general way, it may be said that Cimabue showed himself forcible in his paintings, as especially in heads of aged or strongly characterized men; and, if the then existing development of art had allowed of this, he might have had it in him to express the beautiful as well. He was the first painter who wrote upon his paintings – as for instance, around the head of Christ in a picture of the Crucifixion, the words addressed to Mary, *Woman, behold your son.*

Other paintings still extant by Cimabue are the following: In the academy of Arts in Florence, a *Madonna and Child*, with eight angels, and some prophets in niches – better than the Rucellai picture in composition and study of nature, but more archaic in type, and the colour now spoiled (this work was painted for the Badia of S. Trinita, Florence); in the National Gallery, London, a *Madonna and Child with Angels*, which came

◀ **Cimabue,**
Maestà (Ognissanti Madonna), 1305-1310.
Tempera on wood, 325 x 204 cm.
Galleria degli Uffizi, Florence.

▼ **Cimabue,**
Saint Francis (detail).
Museo della Porziuncola, Church
of Santa Maria degli Angeli, Assisi.

▼ **Cimabue,**
Saint Francis, detail from The Virgin and Child with Angels and Saint Francis, c. 1280-1283. Fresco.
Right transept, Lower Basilica of San Francesco, Assisi.

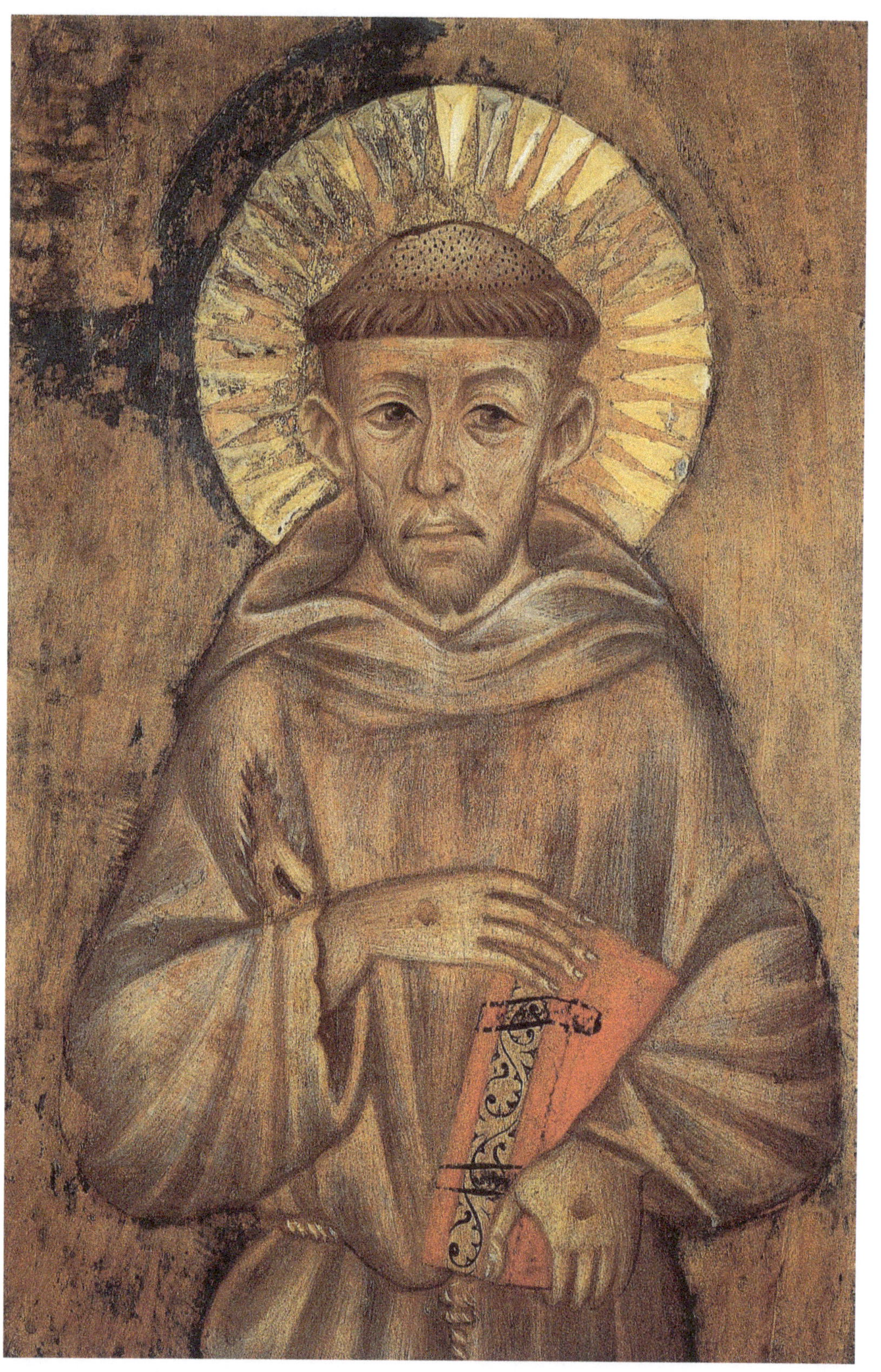

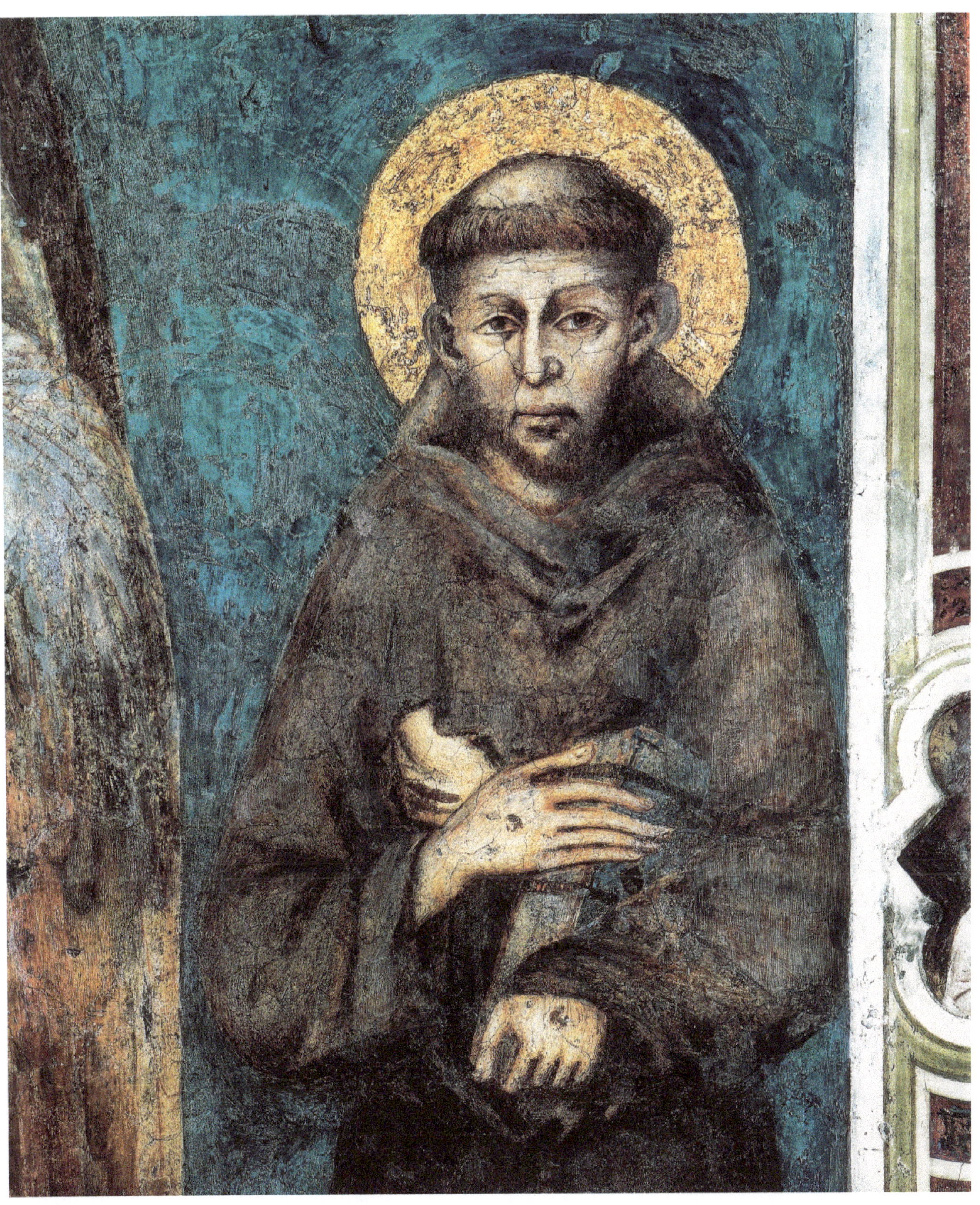

from the Ugo Bakli collection, and had probably once been in the church of S. Frencesco, Pisa. In the lower church of the Basilica of S. Francesco at Assisi, Cimabue, succeeding Giunta da Pisa, probably adorned the south transept - painting a colossal *Virgin and Child between four Angels,* above the altar of the Conception, and a large figure of *St. Francis* .In the upper church, north transept, he has the *Saviour Enthroned and some Angels* and on the central ceiling of the transept, the *Four Evangelists with Angels.* Many other works in both the lower and the upper church have been ascribed to Cimbabue, but with very scanty evidence; even the above-named, can be assigned to him only as a matter of probability.

From Assisi, Cimabue returned to Florence. In the closing years of his life he was appointed capomaestro of the mosaics of the cathedral of Pisa , and was afterwards, hardly a year before his death, joined with Arnolfo di Cambio as architect for the cathedral of Florence. In Pisa he executed a Majesty in the apse, *Christ in glory between the Virgin and John the Evangelist,* a mosaic, now much damaged, which stamps him as the leading artist of his time in that material. This was probably the last Work that he produced.

The debt which art owes to Cimabue is not limited to his own performances. He was the master of Giotto, whom (such at least is the tradition) he found a shepherd boy of ten, in the pastures of Vespignano, drawing with a coal on a slate the figure of a lamb. Cimabue

took him to Florence, and instructed him in the art; and after his death Giotto occupied a house which had belonged to his master in the Via del Cocomero.

It has always been supposed that the bodily semblance of Cimabue is preserved to us in a portrait figure by Simon Memmi painted in the Capella degli Spagnoli, in S. Maria Novella, a thin hooded face in profile, with a small beard, reddish and ponted. This is, however, extremely dubious. Simone Martini of Siena (commonly called Memmi) was born in 1234, and would therefore have been about nineteen years of age when Cimabue died; it is not certain that he painted the work in question, or that the figure represents Cimabue. The Florentine master is spoken of by a nearly contemporary commentator on Dante as "arrogant and scornful" that if anyone or he himself, found a fault in any work of his, however, cherished till then, he would abandon it in disgust. This, however, to a modern mind, looks more like an aspiring and fastidious desire for perfection than any such form of "arrogance and scorn" as blemishes a man's character. Giovanni Cimabue was buried in the cathedral of Florence, S. Maria del Fiore.

Cimabue, ▶
Saint John the Evangelist, c. 1301-1302.
Mosaic.
Apse, Cathedral of Pisa, Pisa.

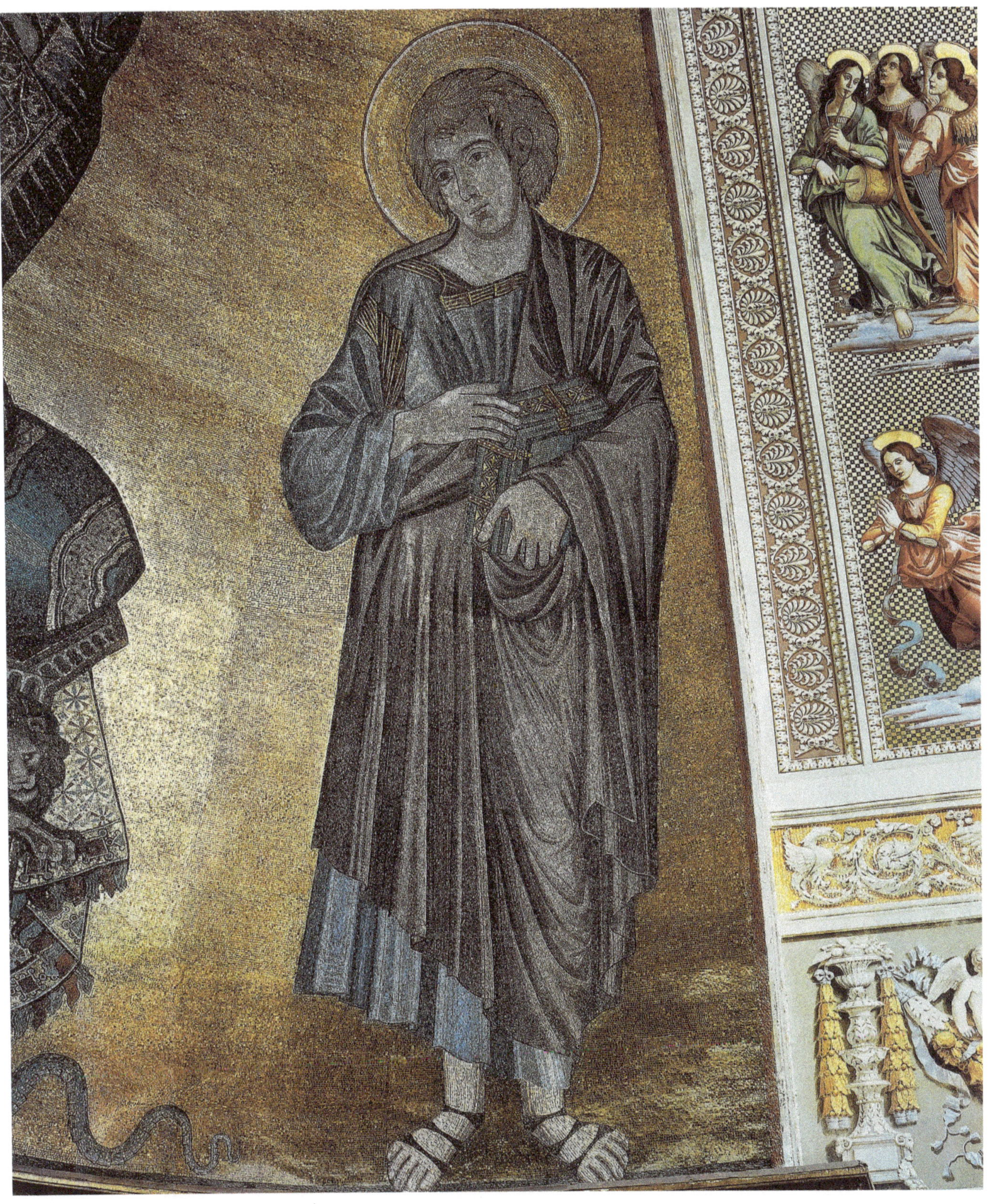

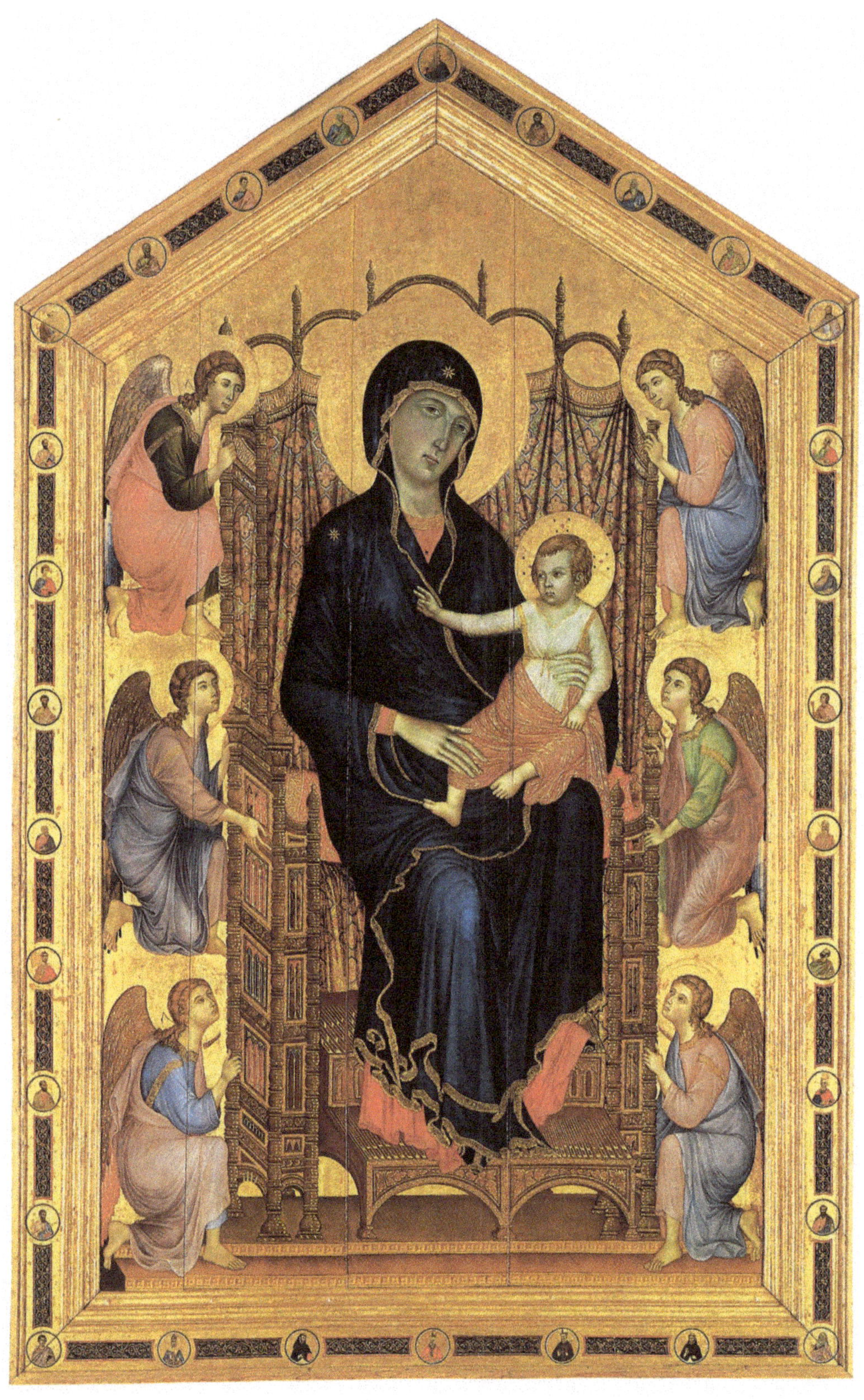

DUCCIO DI BUONINSEGNA

c. 1255-c. 1318

Another Sienese painter was Duccio, who painted from 1282, twenty years before the death of Cimabue, until around 1339, and "whose influence on the progress of art was unquestionably great". To this painter was allotted, in the year 1308, the task of painting the great altarpiece for the beautiful Cathedral of Siena, dedicated to the Virgin Mary. The high altar then stood in the centre of the church, the panel was painted on both sides, as it was to be seen both from in front o and behind the altar. On one side, Duccio represented the history of Christ in 27 small compartments, beginning with the *Annunciation* and ending with the *Crucifixion*, which forms the largest and principal subject. On the other side of the panel was represented the *Madonna and Child* enthroned, on each side six prophets and ten adoring angels, and lower down, on each side, five saints — in total 44 figures.

When finished, this picture was carried in a grand procession, attended by music and rejoicing crowds, to its place in the Cathedral. In 1506, it was removed. The panel was afterwards sawed through into two parts: one side (the *Madonna*) now hangs in the chapel of Sant' Ansano, to the left of the choir; the other (the *Life of Christ*) on the right hand, opposite. They are counted among the most precious monuments of early art. The predella, which was beneath the *Madonna*, contained, as usual, small subjects from the history of the Virgin Mary; these, five in number, are now in the sacristy of the Cathedral. Besides this great altarpiece, only one undoubted picture by Duccio is known to exist.

In October 1308, Duccio declared himself ready to undertake the picture of the high altar. He went into harness at once and diligently proceeded to fulfil his contract. Weeks, months, a year spent in continuous labor had not brought the vast and difficult work to completion, but, on 9 June 1310, it was finished and transported amidst public rejoicings from Duccio's shop in the Casa de' Muciatti, outside the gate Stalloreggi, to its place in the cathedral. Business was entirely suspended on this festive occasion; all the shops of Siena were closed. The archbishop headed the procession of clergy and friars; the "Nine" of the government, the officers of the Commune, the menfolk followed with tapers in their hands, and

◀ **Duccio di Buoninsegna,**
Madonna Rucellai, 1285.
Tempera and gold on panel, 450 x× 290 cm.
Galleria degli Uffizi, Florence.

last came the women and children. All marched with great solemnity to the sound of trumpets and ringing of bells, the highest in rank or dignity clustering about the picture, and, undoubtedly, Duccio himself enjoying the popular enthusiasm and clamour.

Duccio became the hero of the hour. He deserved it. On a surface fourteen feet long and seven feet high, he had placed the Virgin, seated with the infant Christ in a vast throne, richly covered with tapestry and ornaments. This was not, however, an altarpiece intended to be seen from one side only; it was to be visible from both sides. So having depicted, on the one hand, the *Maesta*, Duccio divided the surface of the opposite face into 38 parts, devoting it to the two principal scenes of the story he intended to illustrate, which was that of the *Passion*.

The vehemence of the early period is still marked in the *Magdalen*, whose expression is more of grief than longing. Duccio, in fact, repeated the typical episode of the *Barberini Exultet* at the very period when pilgrims to Assisi might admire the conception of the subject which Giotto had left there. Nothing finer was considered to have been produced in the old time than the *Maries at the Sepulchre*, whether considered in reference to type or to form and action. Duccio could therefore have done no better than to copy it, as he did.

The *Entrance into Jerusalem*, a double panel at the left lower angle of the altarpiece, opens the story of the *Passion*, and is a careful imitation of the subject, a tasteful miniature in color and execution. The last scene of the *Passion*, equal in size to the preceding but occupying the centre of the altarpiece, is the *Crucifixion*, in which Duccio may again be compared with Giotto.

If Duccio left pictures behind at Pisa, Lucca, or Pistoia they have perished. One of Duccio's finest productions, a *Crucifixion, Virgin and Child* and attendant episodes, second only in prominence to the altarpiece of the Duomo of Siena, can be found in the Royal Collections in Hampton Court. Another picture of interest by Duccio is a triptych now in the National Gallery in London. In New York, there is also a *Madonna and Child* in the Metropolitan Museum of Art, while other works ascribed to Duccio, including polyptychs, portable altarpieces, and stained-glass windows adorn numerous museums in Europe, as well as churches in Italy.

Duccio di Buoninsegna, ▶
The Temptation of Christ on the Mountain, 1308-1311.
Tempera on wood, 43.2 x 46 cm.
The Frick Collection, New York.

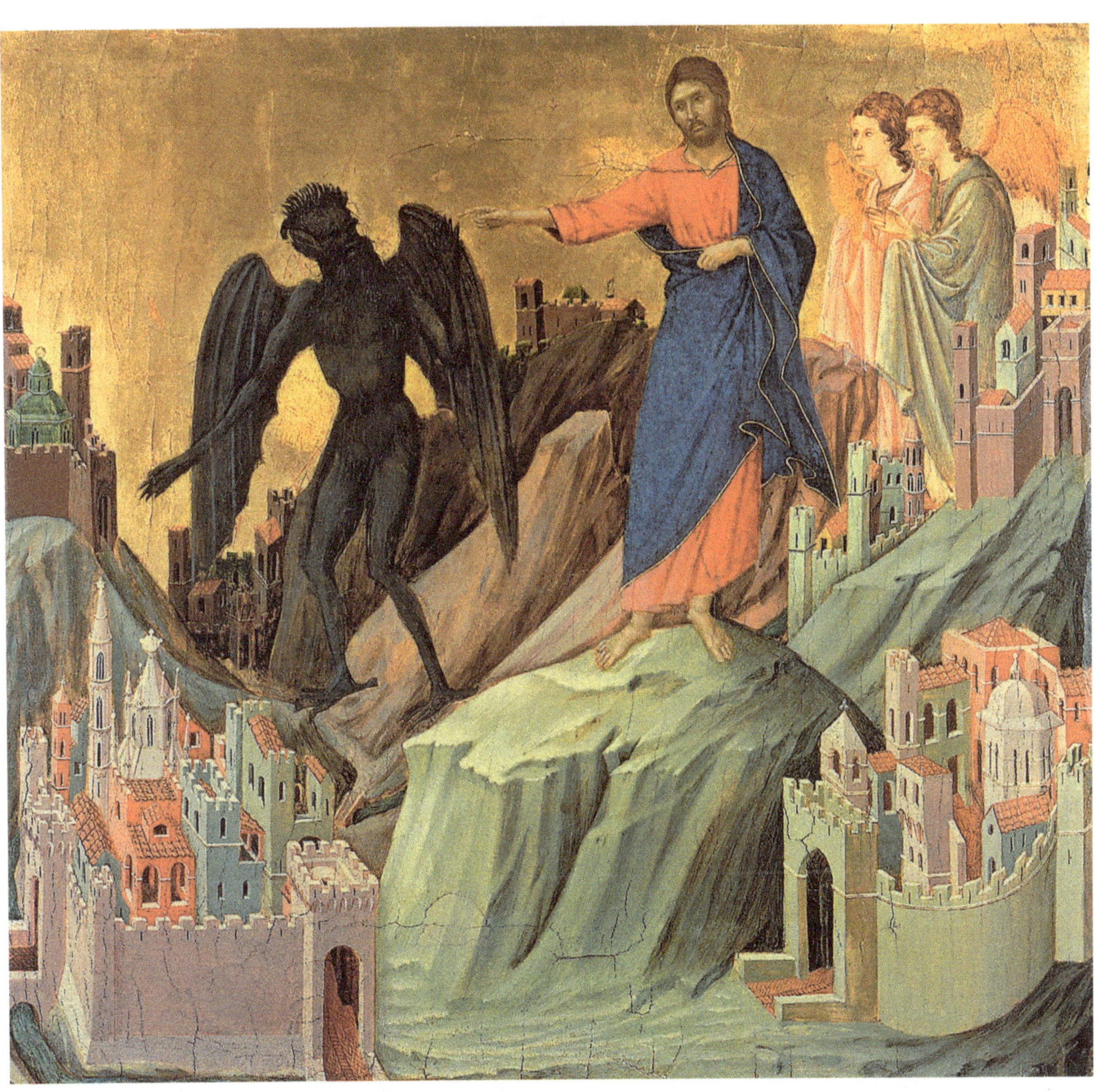

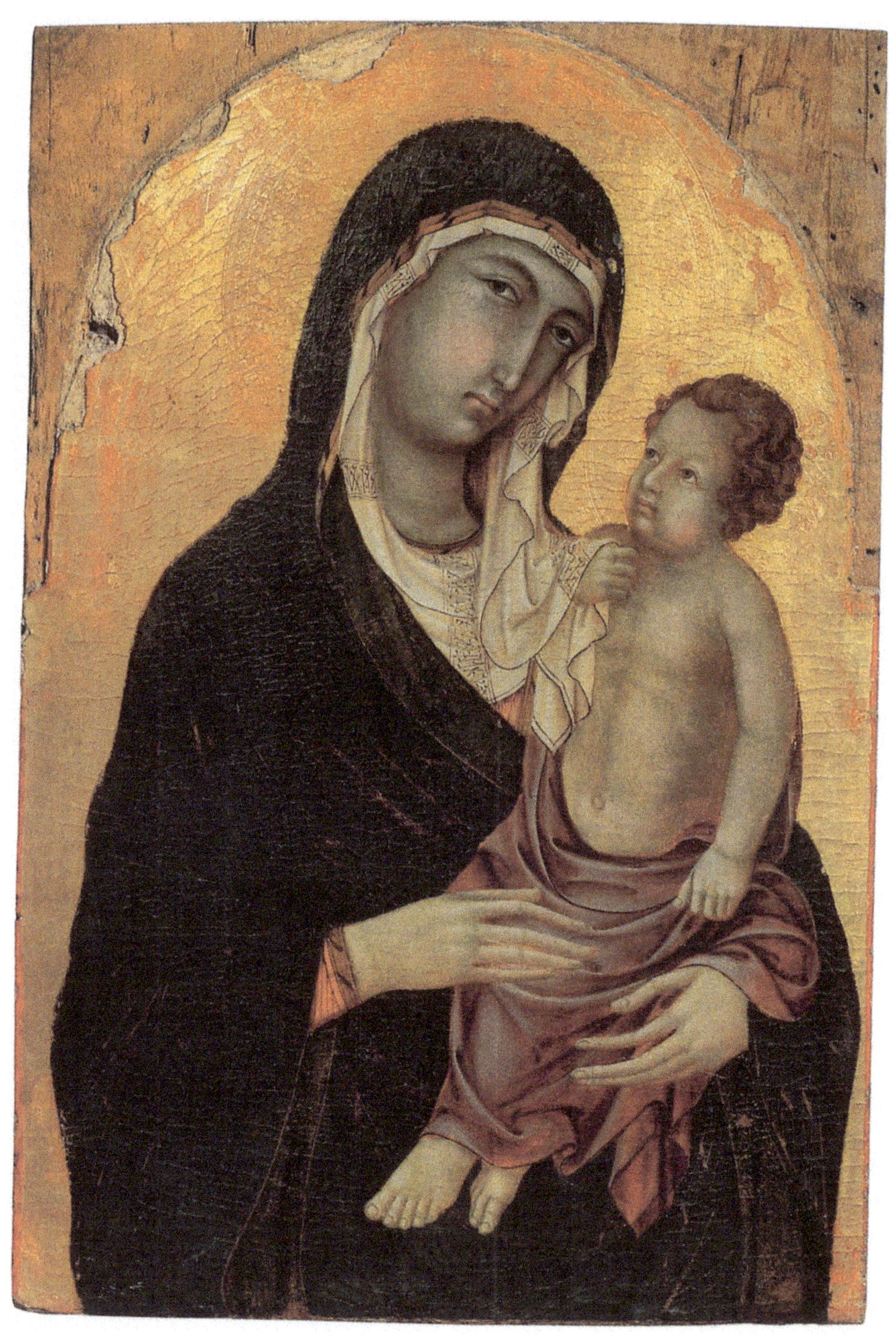

▲ **Ugolino di Nerio**, *The Virgin and Child*, c. 1315-1320.
Tempera on wood panel, 69 x 47 cm. Musée du Louvre, Paris.

UGOLINO DI NERIO

1280(?)-1349

Contemporary of and patriarch of the Sienese school along with Duccio, is Ugolino, respected by no authentic records, and of whom only one picture has an inscription, without a date. It was principally in Siena that we must seek the vestiges of an artist who not only followed the old style like Duccio, but who exaggerated it even more than that master. It is in Florence that Ugolino worked most and there in which his only inscribed picture occupied a place in the church of St. Croce, and that a number of works in his peculiar manner are preserved. Ugolino, during his stay in Florence, was employed by the Franciscans of St. Croce to paint a picture for the high altar of the church, and as Arnolfo did not begin the edifice until 1294, we may assume that Ugolino's work was subsequent to that date.

The altarpiece of St. Croce was a truly Sienese production in form, with the *Virgin and Child Enthroned* in the centre, saints and apostles in higher courses, scenes from the *Passion* on the pediment, and the whole work signed *UGOLINO DE SENIS ME PINXIT*. Like most pictures of that time, Ugolino's altarpiece was withdrawn from its place of honor, and stowed away. It remained unheeded for centuries in the dormitory of the convent, where Delia Valle saw it, and, having been sold for a song, found its way in fragments to the Ottley collection, which now constitute some of the eleven panels in the National Gallery in London. Others can also be found in the Cleveland Museum of Art, the Louvre, and in the Church of Misericordia in San Casciano, Italy. In these, a color and technical execution like those of Duccio, Simone, and other Sienese, may be traced. The figures are long and bony, the movements more vehement and exaggerated than those of Duccio.

The colossal *Madonna* in the tabernacle of Orsanmichele, with the infant Christ on her knee caressing her and holding a bird, and the glory of eight angels, of whom two in front wave censers, have characteristics of the close of the fourteenth century and something of Sienese peculiarity. Lorenzo Monaco is much more likely to have painted them than Ugolino. Vasari does not pretend that Ugolino produced a *Virgin* on panel at Orsanmichele, but that he executed it on a pilaster — a statement in which he is confirmed by the testimony of Villani.

A *Coronation of the Virgin*, with the usual choirs of angels and saints about the throne, once exhibited in the Galleria dell'Accademia in Florence under Ugolino's name, was supposed to be the original referred to by Vasari as having been painted for the high altar of Santa Maria Novella. But the style was of a less developed artist, of the time of Agnolo Gaddi.

Vasari finally alludes to a *Crucified Christ*, a *Magdalen* and *Evangelist*, with two pairs of kneeling monks at the sides, executed by Ugolino for the chapel of Ridolfo de' Bardi at St. Croce. No such picture exists there now.

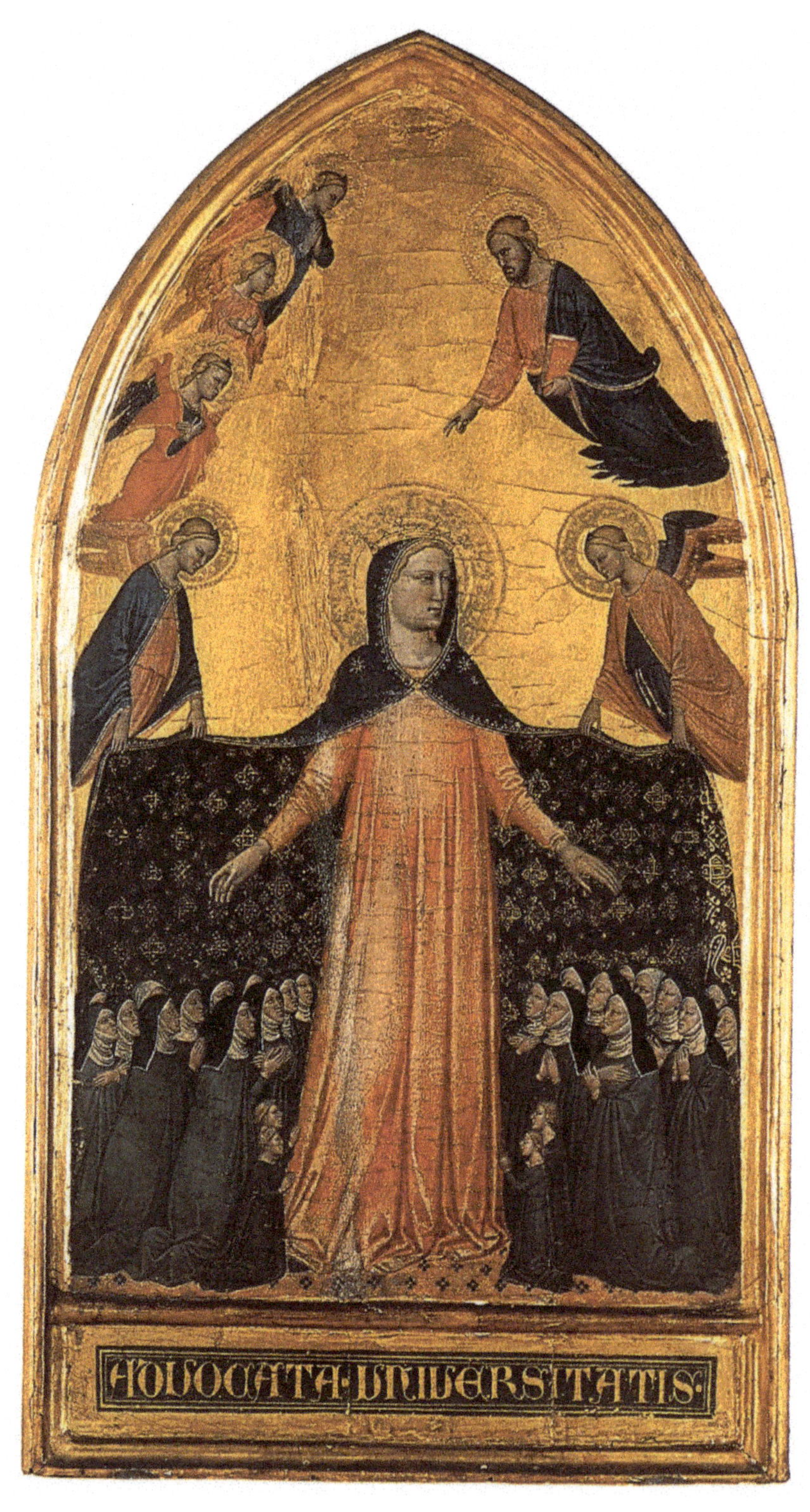

▲ **Segna di Bonaventura**, *The Master of the Misericordia, Madonna of Misericordia (Mercy), c. 1373.* Tempera on wood, 63 x 34 cm. Galleria dell'Accademia, Florence.

SEGNA DI BONAVENTURA

Active c. 1298-1331

Another painter of the early school in Siena who remained partial to the oldest forms, and who is consequently related to Ugolino more so than to Simone or the Lorenzetti, was Segna di Bonaventura, who is said to have finished a picture for the Biccherna in 1305-1306, part of which, along with his signature, can be found in the Pinacoteca Nazionale in Siena. A better and previously unknown example of this master is a *Majesty*, with the usual garland of angels surrounding the back and arms of the throne, and four miniature donors kneeling in the foreground, in the church of Castiglione Fiorentino, which is no great distance from Arezzo.

The infant Christ, standing, draws together a yellowish veil that covers his mother's head, and with his left hand keeps his own little red mantle around his neck. A certain majesty marks the Virgin's form and proportion. Her face, though of no new type, but oval, broad at the brow and small at the chin, is enlivened by large but regular eyes. Thin long-fingered hands are an additional peculiarity of the Sienese, thumbs resting on no muscular base and having no apparent bond with the rest of the parts. Aged features, yet plump cheeks and swelling lips, a high round forehead, gazing eyes and a round, balled nose are marked in Christ, whose nude form betrays an incomplete anatomical study by Segna. The toes are lined as if on lifeless blocks in the old style; but the drapery is broad in fold and richly shot with gold lines. The forms and features of the celestial messengers, of whom six surround the Virgin, are old and ugly, the eyes being large and open, the lower lips overhanging and the necks slender and long.

At the top of the stairs leading into the convent of St. Francesco in Castel Florentine, a not ungraceful *Madonna* in Segna's manner may be seen. There is, however, some affectation of singularity in the Virgin's manner of holding the infant Christ. Her hands are between his legs, and the frame of the Child is unusually large and disproportioned.

A large crucifix in the Abbey of St. Fiora at Arezzo reveals the same hand, and the star-formed panels at the base summit of the cross are like those of the crucifix at the Servi in Siena. Segna's inscribed works at the Pinacoteca Nazionale in Siena are four panels representing the *Virgin, St. Paul, John Evangelist, Bernard* and another saint, all painted in the lean character specific to the master, fine in drapery, and not without an intention of grace in the movement of the Virgin. Time has, unfortunately, proved injurious to the surfaces which represent flesh. In the National Gallery of London, there is a well-preserved panel by Segna of the crucifixion which can be seen between the Virgin and St. John. Two panels in the Pinacoteca Nazionale di Siena which represent S.S. Ansano and Galgano, were originally executed by Segna for the Palazzo Pubblico in 1314.

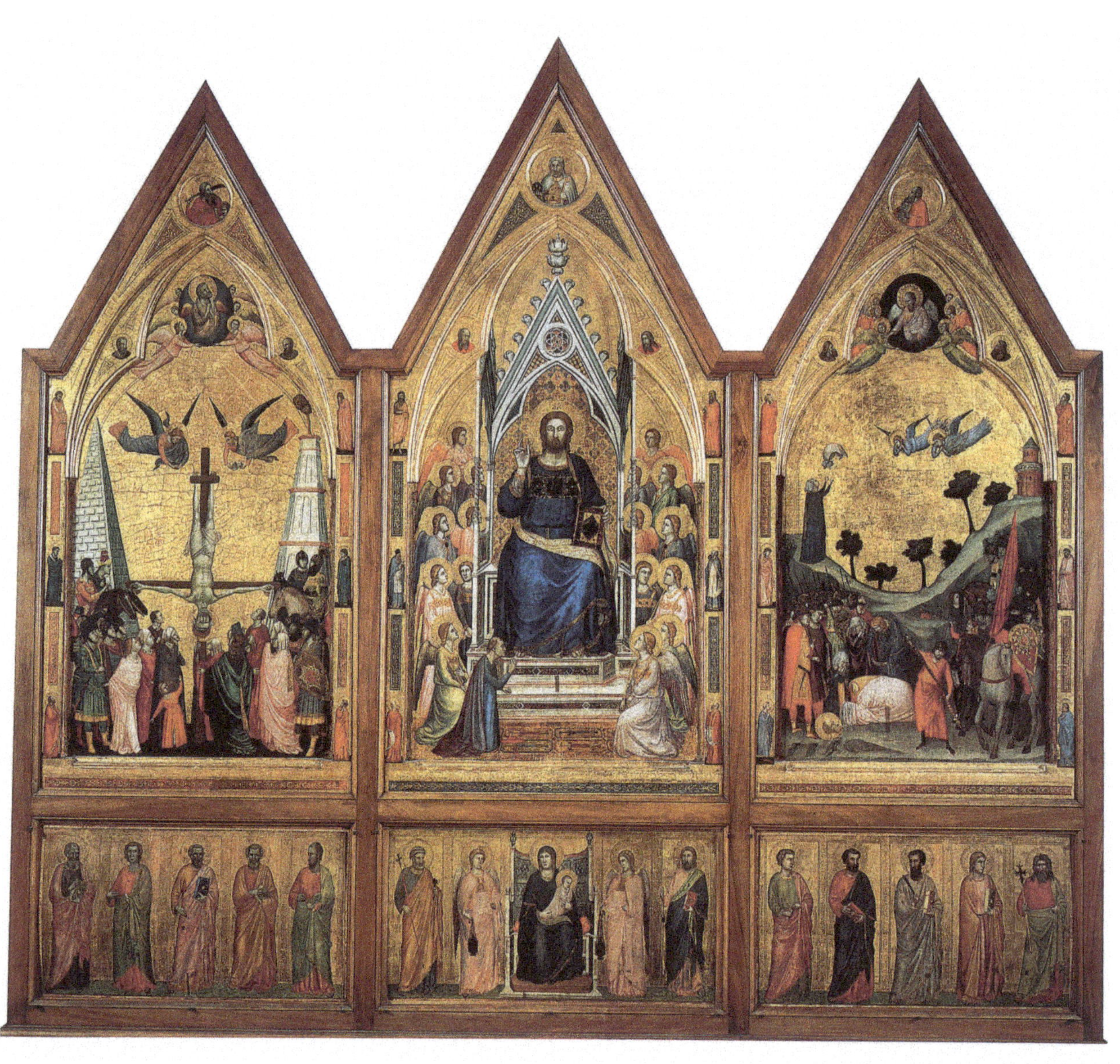

GIOTTO DI BONDONE

1267-1337

No single human being of whom we read has exercised, in any particular department of art, a more immediate, wide, and lasting influence. The total change in the direction and character of art must in all human probability have taken place sooner or later, since all the influences of that wonderful period of regeneration were tending towards it. Then did architecture struggle as it was from the Byzantine into the Gothic forms, like a mighty plant putting forth its rich foliage and shooting up towards the sky; then did the speech of people — the vulgar tongues, as they were called — begin to assume their present structure and become the medium through which beauty, love, action, feeling and thought were to be uttered and immortalised; and then arose Giotto, the instrument through which his own beautiful art was to become one of the great interpreters of the human soul, with all its "infinite" of feelings and faculties, and of human life in all its multifarious aspects.

Around the year 1289, when Cimabue was already old and at the height of his fame, as he was riding in the valley of Vespignano about fourteen miles from Florence, his attention was attracted by a boy who was herding sheep. While his flocks were feeding around, he appeared intently drawing the figure of one of his sheep as it was quietly grazing before him on a smooth fragment of slate with a bit of pointed stone. Cimabue rode up, and, looking with astonishment at the performance of the untutored boy, asked him if he would go with him and learn. The boy replied that he was indeed willing if his father were content with the arrangement. His father, a herdsman of the valley by the name of Bondone, gladly consented to the wish of the noble stranger, and Giotto subsequently became Cimabue's apprentice.

Giotto was around twelve or fourteen years old when he was taken into the house of Cimabue. For his instruction in those branches of polite learning necessary to an artist, his protector placed him under the tuition of Brunetto Latini, who was also the pedagogue of Dante. When, at the age of 26, Giotto lost his friend and master, he was already an accomplished man as well as a celebrated painter.

The first recorded performance of Giotto was a painting on the wall of the Palazzo deli' Podesta, or council chamber of Florence, in which the portraits of Dante, Brunetto Latini, Corso Donati, and others

◀ **Giotto di Bondone,**
Stefaneschi Polyptych, c. 1330.
Tempera on panel, 220 x 245 cm.
Pinacoteca Vaticana, The Vatican, Rome.

were introduced. They were soon afterwards plastered or whitewashed over during the triumph of the enemies of Dante; for ages, though known to exist, they were lost and buried from sight. The hope of recovering these most interesting portraits had long been entertained and various attempts were made at different times without success. Finally, as late as 1840, they were brought to light by the perseverance and enthusiasm of Bezzi and Kirkup, assisted by a subscription among the English and American residents and visitors then in Florence. On comparing the head of Dante painted when he was about thirty, prosperous and distinguished in his native city, with the later portraits of him as an exile, worn, wasted, and embittered by misfortune, disappointment, and wounded pride, the difference of expression is as touching as the identity being featured is unequivocal.

The attention which Giotto seems to have given to all natural forms and appearances in his childhood showed itself in his earlier pictures; he was the first to whom it occurred to group his personages into something like a situation and to give to their attitudes and features the expression adapted to it. Thus, in a very early picture of the *Annunciation*, he gave the Virgin a look of fear; in another, painted some time afterwards, of the *Presentation in the Temple*, he made the infant Christ shrink from the priest and turn to extend his little arms to his mother — the first attempt at that species of grace and naïveté of expression that was later to be carried to perfection by Raphael. These and other works painted in his native city, so astonished his fellow citizens and all who beheld their beauty and novelty that they seem to have pined for

adequate words in which to express the excess of their delight and admiration.

In the church of Santa Croce in Florence, Giotto painted a *Coronation of the Virgin*, replete with choirs of angels and a multitude of saints on either side. In the refectory he painted the *Last Supper*, also still remaining; a grand, solemn, simple composition, which, as a first endeavor to give variety of expression and attitude to a number of persons — all seated, and all but two actuated by a similar feeling — can still be regarded as extraordinary. In a chapel of the church of the Carmine in Florence, he painted a series of pictures from the life of John the Baptist. These were destroyed by fire in 1771; but, luckily, an English engraver studying in Florence, named Patch, had previously made accurate drawings from them, which he engraved and published.

Upon hearing of his marvelous skill, Pope Boniface VIII invited Giotto to Rome and there he completed many works which raised his fame higher and higher; among them, for the ancient Basilica of St. Peter's, the famous colossal mosaic of the *Navicella*, or the *Barca* as it is sometimes called. It represents a ship containing the Disciples on a tempestuous sea, the winds, personified as demons, rage around it. Above are the fathers of the Old Testament; on the right stands Christ, raising Peter

Giotto di Bondone, ▶
St. Francis receiving the Stigmata, predella: The Dream of Innocent III; The Pope approving the order's status, Saint Francis preaching the birds, c. 1295-1300.
Tempera on wood, 313 x 163 cm.
Musée du Louvre, Paris.

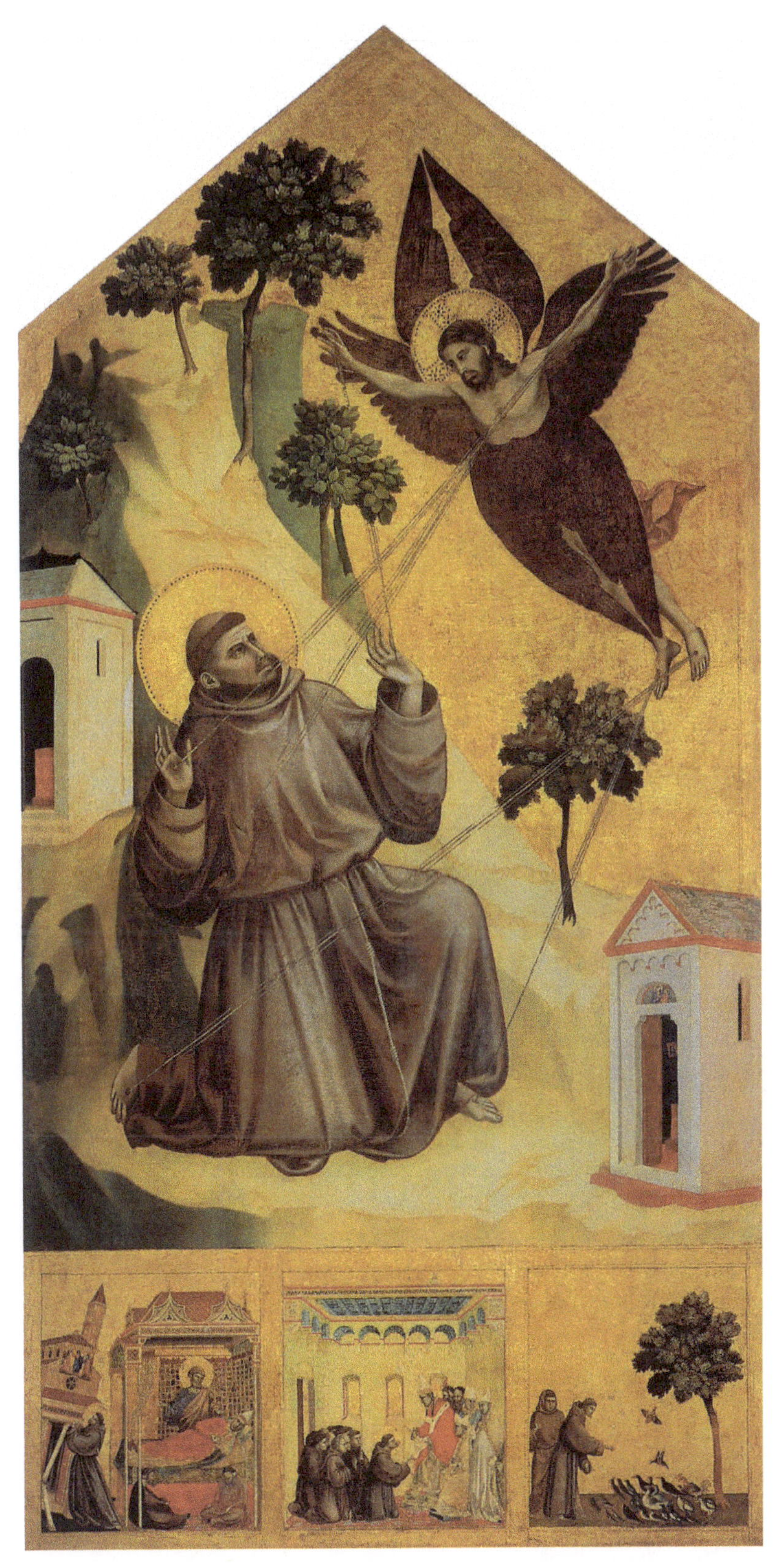

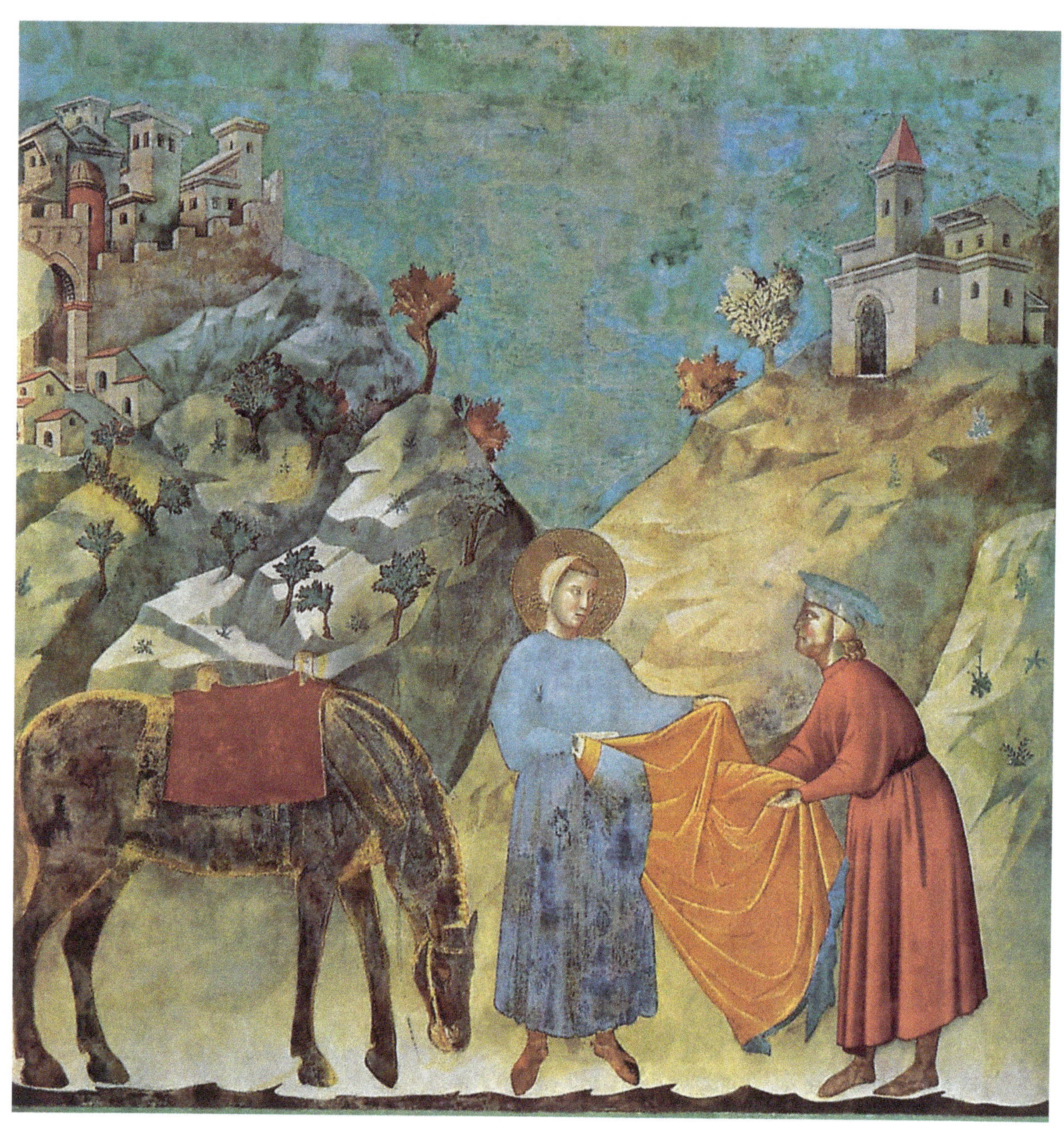

▲ **Giotto di Bondone**,
St. Francis Giving his Cloak to a Poor Man, 1296-1299.
Fresco, 270 x 230 cm.
Upper Basilica of San Francesco, Assisi.

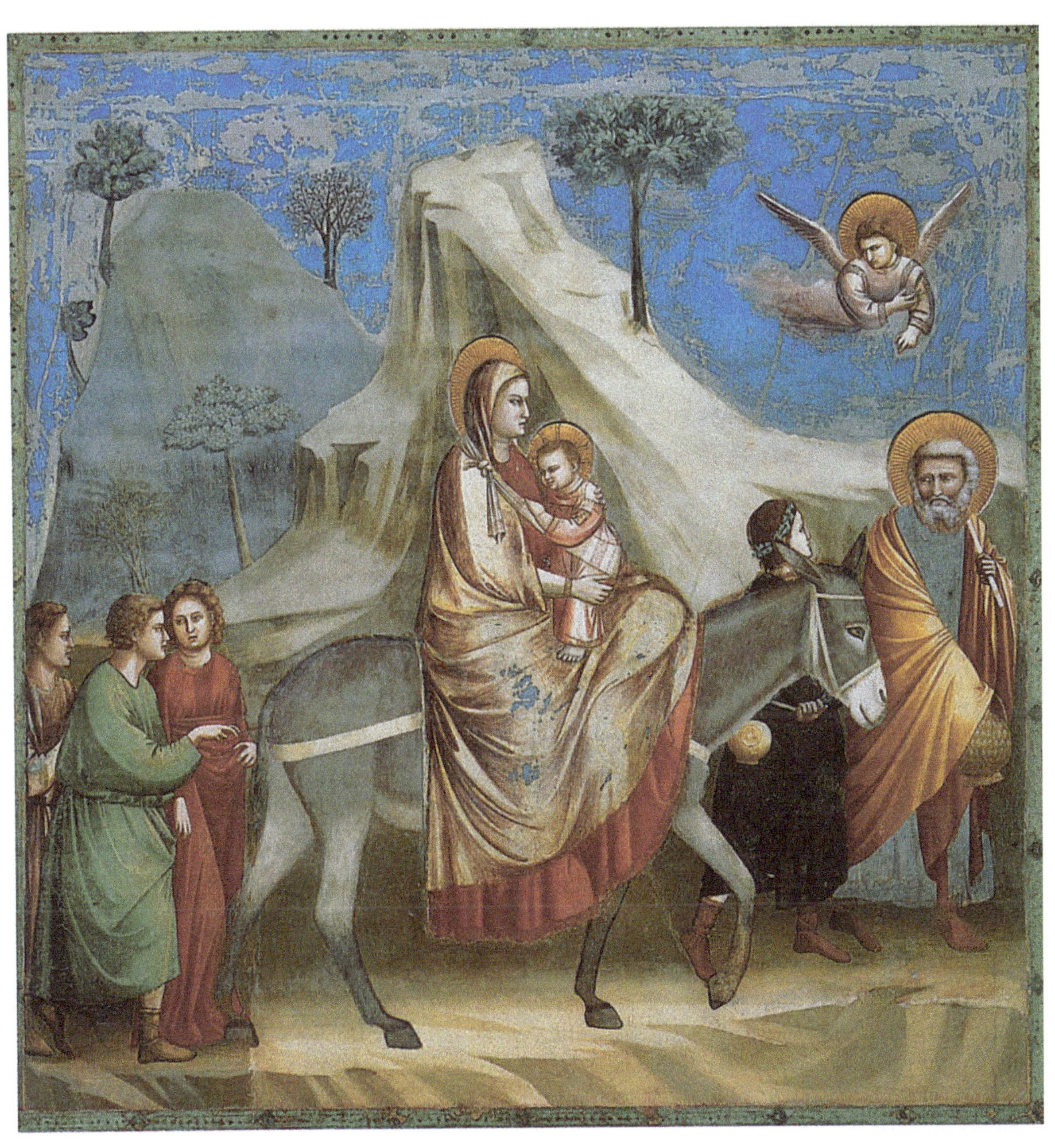

▲ **Giotto di Bondone**,
The Flight to Egypt, 1303-1305.
Fresco, 200 x 185 cm.
Cappella degli Scrovegni all'Arena (Arena Chapel), Padua.

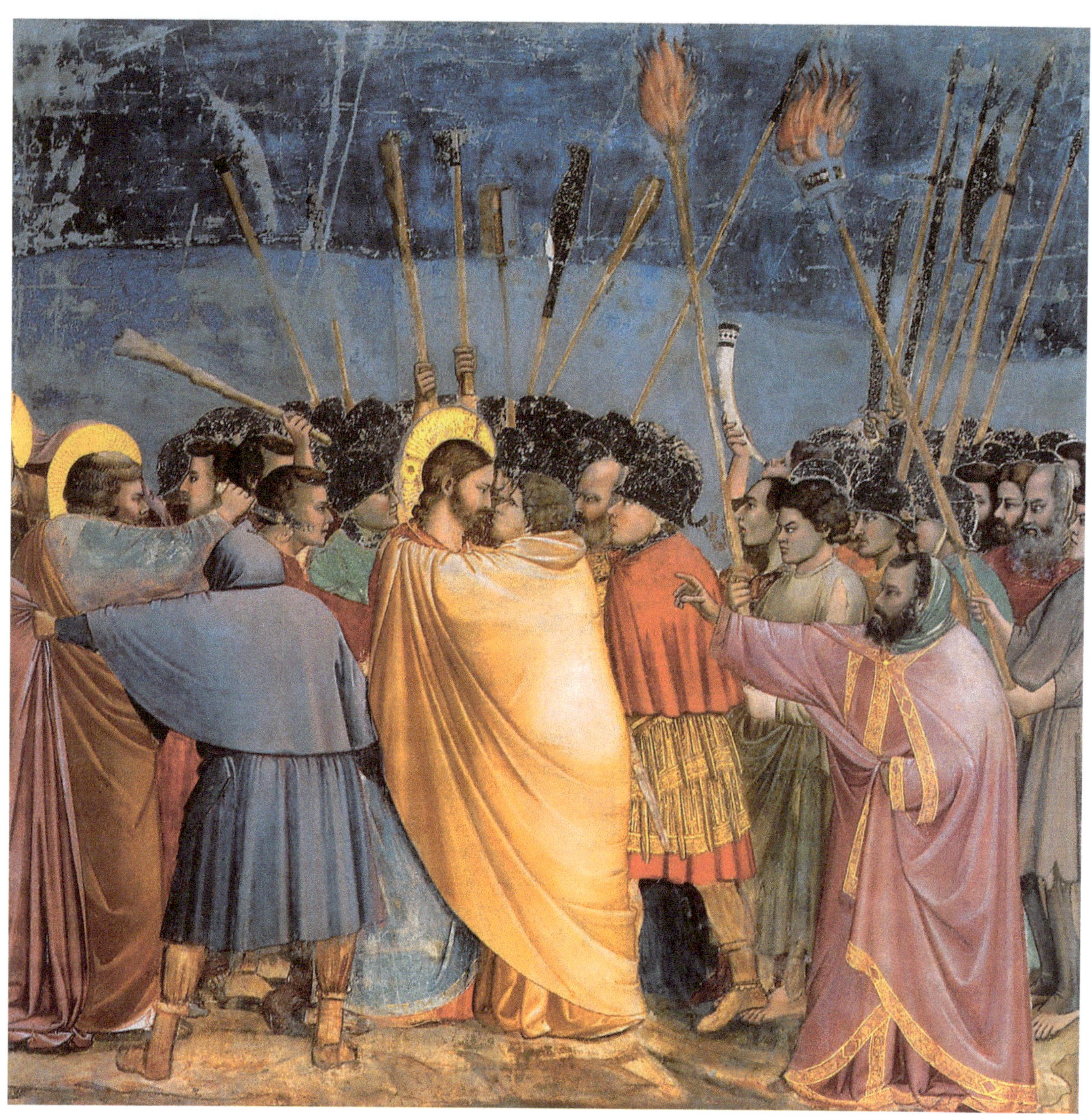

from the waves. The subject has an allegorical significance, denoting the troubles and triumphs of the Church. This mosaic has often changed its situation, and has been restored again and again, leaving nothing of Giotto's work but the original composition. It is now in the vestibule of St. Peter's at Rome over the arch facing the principal gate.

For the same Pope Boniface, Giotto painted the *Institution of the Jubilee of 1300*, which still exists in the portico of the Lateran in Rome. In Padua, he painted the chapel of the Arena with frescoes inspired by Christ and the Virgin in 50 square compartments. In Padua, Giotto met his friend Dante; the influence of one great genius on another is strongly exemplified in some of his succeeding works and particularly in his next grand performance, the frescoes in the church of Assisi. In the lower church, and immediately over the tomb of St. Francis, Giotto represented the three "vows of the Order" — *Poverty*, *Chastity*, and *Obedience*; and in the fourth compartment, the Saint enthroned and glorified amidst the host of Heaven. The invention of the allegories under which Giotto has represented the vows of the Saint, — his *Marriage with Poverty*, Chastity seated in her rocky fortress and Obedience with the curb and yoke — are ascribed by a tradition to Dante. Giotto also painted, in the Campo Santo at Pisa, the whole *History of Job*, of which only some fragments remain.

◀ **Giotto di Bondone**,
The Betrayal of Christ, c. 1305.
Fresco, 185 x 200 cm.
Cappella degli Scrovegni all'Arena (Arena Chapel), Padua.

By the time Giotto attained his thirtieth year he had reached such hitherto unknown excellence in art; his celebrity was so universal that every city and every small sovereign in Italy contended for the honor of his presence and his pencil, tempting him with the promise of rich rewards. For the Lords of Arezzo, of Rimini and Ravenna, and for the Duke of Milan, he executed many works, almost all of which have been lost.

For Malatesta di Rimini, the father of Francesca's husband, he painted the portrait of the prince in a boat with his companions and a company of mariners, among which, Vasari tells us, was the figure of a sailor, who, turning around with his hand before his face, is in the act of spitting in the sea, so life-like as to strike beholders with amazement. The latter has perished; but the figure of the thirsty man stooping to drink in one of the frescoes in Assisi still remains to show the kind of excellence through which Giotto excited such admiration in his contemporaries: a power of imitation, a truth in the expression of natural actions, and feelings to which painting had yet reached.

Around 1327, King Robert of Naples wrote to his son, Duke of Calabria, then in Florence. He asked him to send, on any terms, the famous painter Giotto, who accordingly travelled to the court of Naples, stopping on his way in several cities where he left specimens of his skill. There is a *Crucifixion* painted by Giotto in Gaeta, which he completed either on his way to Naples or on his return. In it, he introduced himself kneeling in an attitude of deep devotion and contrition at the foot of the cross: this introduction of portraiture into such a sensitive subject was another innovation, perhaps not so immediately praised as some of his other characteristics. Giotto's feeling for truth and propriety of expression is particularly remarkable in his alteration of the tortuous but popular subject of the crucifix: in the Byzantine school, the sole aim seems to have been to represent physical agony and to render it, by every technique of distortion and exaggeration possible, as terrible and repulsive.

Giotto was the first to soften this painful image by lending an expression of divine resignation, and through greater attention to beauty of form. A crucifixion which he painted became the model for his scholars; it was multiplied by imitation through all of Italy. King Robert received him with great honor and rejoice; being a monarch of singular accomplishments, and fond of the society of cultivated and distinguished men, he soon found that Giotto was not merely a painter, but a man of the world, a man of various acquirements, whose general reputation for wit and vivacity was not unmerited. He would sometimes visit the painter at his work, and, while watching the rapid progress of his pencil, amused himself with the quaint good sense of his discourse. "If I were you, Giotto," said the king to him one very hot day, "I would leave off work and rest myself." "And so would I, sire," replied the painter, "if I were *you!*" The king, apparently in a playful mood, desired him to paint his kingdom, on which Giotto immediately sketched the figure of an ass with a heavy pack-saddle on its back, smelling with an eager air at another pack saddle lying on the ground, on which were a crown and scepter. By this emblem the satirical painter expressed the perceived servility and fickleness of the Neapolitans, and the king at once understood the allusion.

Giotto left Naples around 1328 and returned to his native city with a great increase of wealth and fame. He continued his works with unabated vigor, assisted by his pupils, who attended the most famous school in Italy. Like most of the early Italian artists, he was an architect and sculptor as well as a painter; and his last public work was the exquisitely beautiful *campanile*, or bell-tower, in Florence, for which he made all the designs, even completing the models for the sculpture on the three lower divisions with his own hands. When the emperor Charles V saw this elegant structure, he exclaimed that it ought to be "kept under glass". In the same allegorical taste, Giotto painted many pictures of the "Virtues and Vices", ingeniously invented and rendered with great attention to natural and appropriate expression.

A short time before his death Giotto was invited to Milan by Azzo Visconti. He executed some admirable frescoes in the ancient palace of the dukes of Milan, which have since perished. Finally, having returned to Florence, he soon died — "yielding up his soul to God in the year 1336; and having been," adds Vasari, "no less a good Christian than an excellent painter" he was

Giotto di Bondone, ▶
Cycle of the Life of Joachim (general view), 1303-1305.
Fresco.
Arena Chapel (Cappella degli Scrovegni all'Arena), Padua.

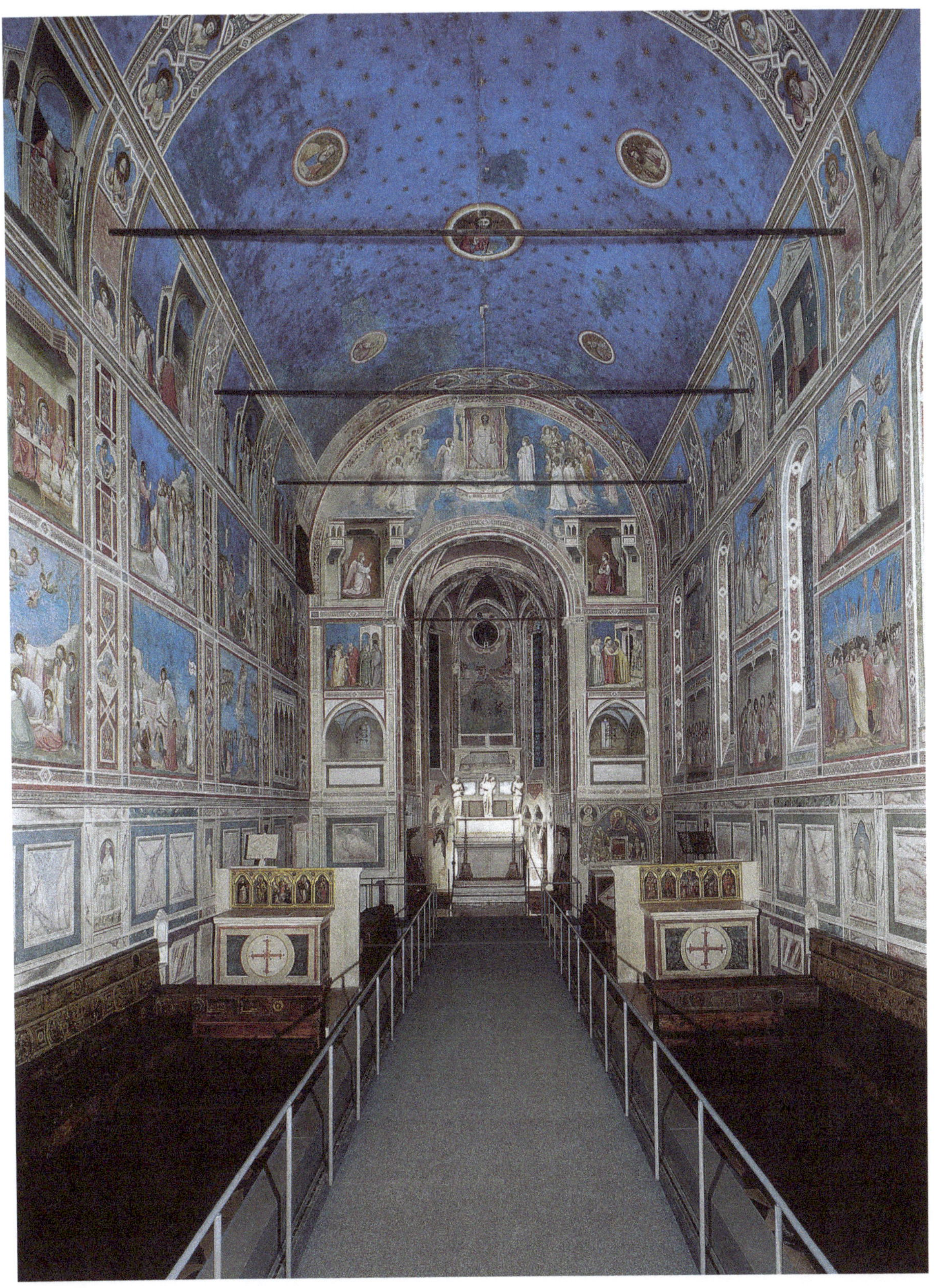

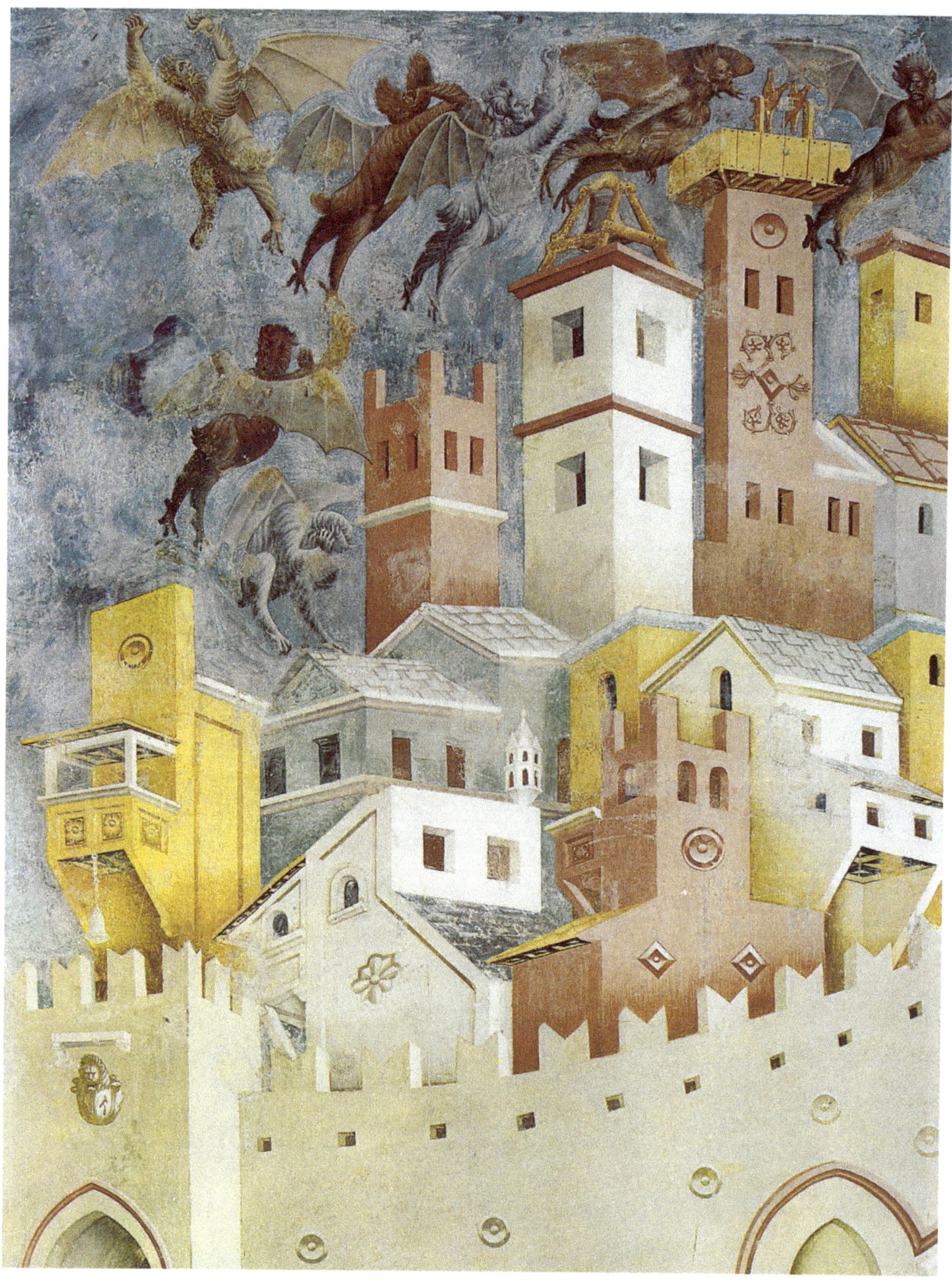

honorably interred in the church of Santa Maria del Fiore, where his master Cimabue had been laid with similar honors 35 years before. Lorenzo de' Medici would later place his effigy in marble above his tomb.

Giotto left four sons and four daughters, but we are not aware of any of his descendants becoming distinguished in art or otherwise. Before we proceed to give some account of the personal character and influence of Giotto, both as a man and an artist, of which many amusing and interesting traits have been handed down to us, we must turn for a moment to reconsider that revolution in art which originated with him — and immediately seized imagination and sympathy, which also, during a whole century, filled Italy and Sicily with disciples formed in the same school and imbued with the same ideas.

All that had been done in painting before Giotto revolved around the imitation of certain existing models and their improvement to a certain point in style of execution was limited by the parameters of preceding examples. The Byzantine types predominated, and, more or less modified, a Madonna in the middle accompanied by a couple of lank saints or angels adjoined on each side; saints bearing symbols or with their names written over their heads and texts of scripture proceeding from

The Demons Chased from Arezzo, c. 1296. Fresco. Main Basilica, Cappella degli Scrovegni all'Arena (Arena Chapel), Padua.

their mouths. Giotto, almost from the beginning of his career, not only deviated from the practice of the older painters, but stood in flagrant opposition to them. He not only improved — he changed; he placed himself on entirely new ground.

For his heads he introduced a new type, exactly reversing the Greek pattern: long-shaped, half-shut eyes, a long, straight nose and a very short chin. The hands are rather delicate, but never accurately drawn, and he could not design feet well, for which reason we generally find those of his men clothed in shoes or sandals wherever it is possible, and those of his women covered with flowing drapery. The management of his draperies is, indeed, particularly characteristic; distinguished by a certain lengthiness and narrowness in the folds, in which there is much taste and simplicity, though, in point of style, as far from the antique as from the complicated severity of the Byzantine models.

It is curious that this peculiar treatment of the drapery, these long perpendicular folds correspond in character with the principles of Gothic architecture. For the stiff, wooden limbs and motionless figures of the Byzantine school, he substituted life, movement, and the look, at least, of flexibility. He seems to have taken his notions of grouping and arrangement from the ancient bas-reliefs; there is a statuesque grace and simplicity in his compositions which reminds us of them. His style of coloring and execution was, like all the rest, an innovation on received methods. His colors were lighter and more roseate than had ever been known; the fluidity by which they were tempered was thinner and easily managed.

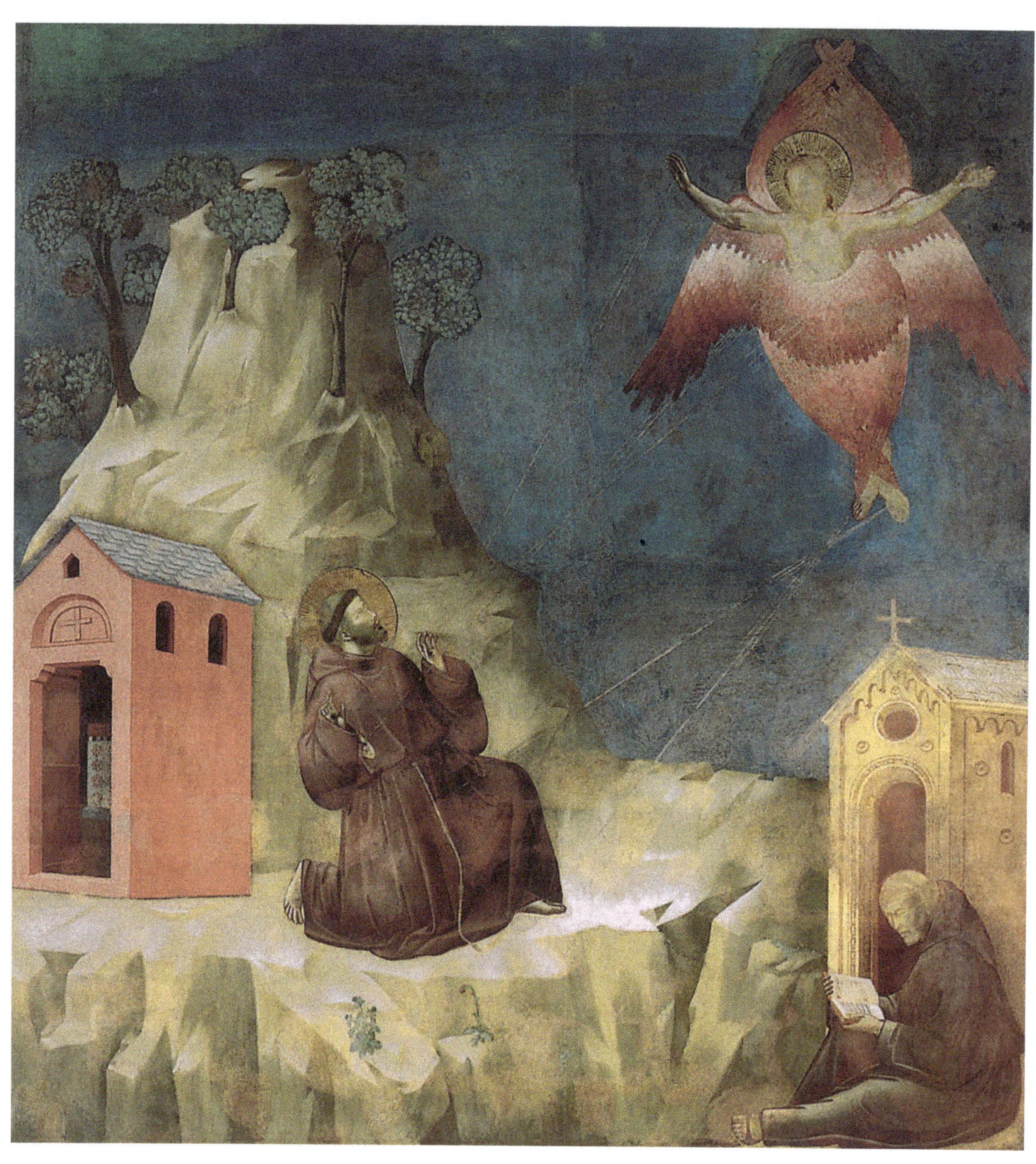

▲ **Giotto di Bondone**, *Cycle of the Life of St. Francis:*
Stigmatisation of St. Francis, 1297-1300.
Fresco, 270 x 230 cm.
Upper Basilica of San Francesco, Assisi.

Giotto di Bondone (?), ▶
The Demons Chased from Arezzo, 1297-1299.
Fresco, 270 x 230 cm.
Upper Basilica of San Francesco, Assisi.

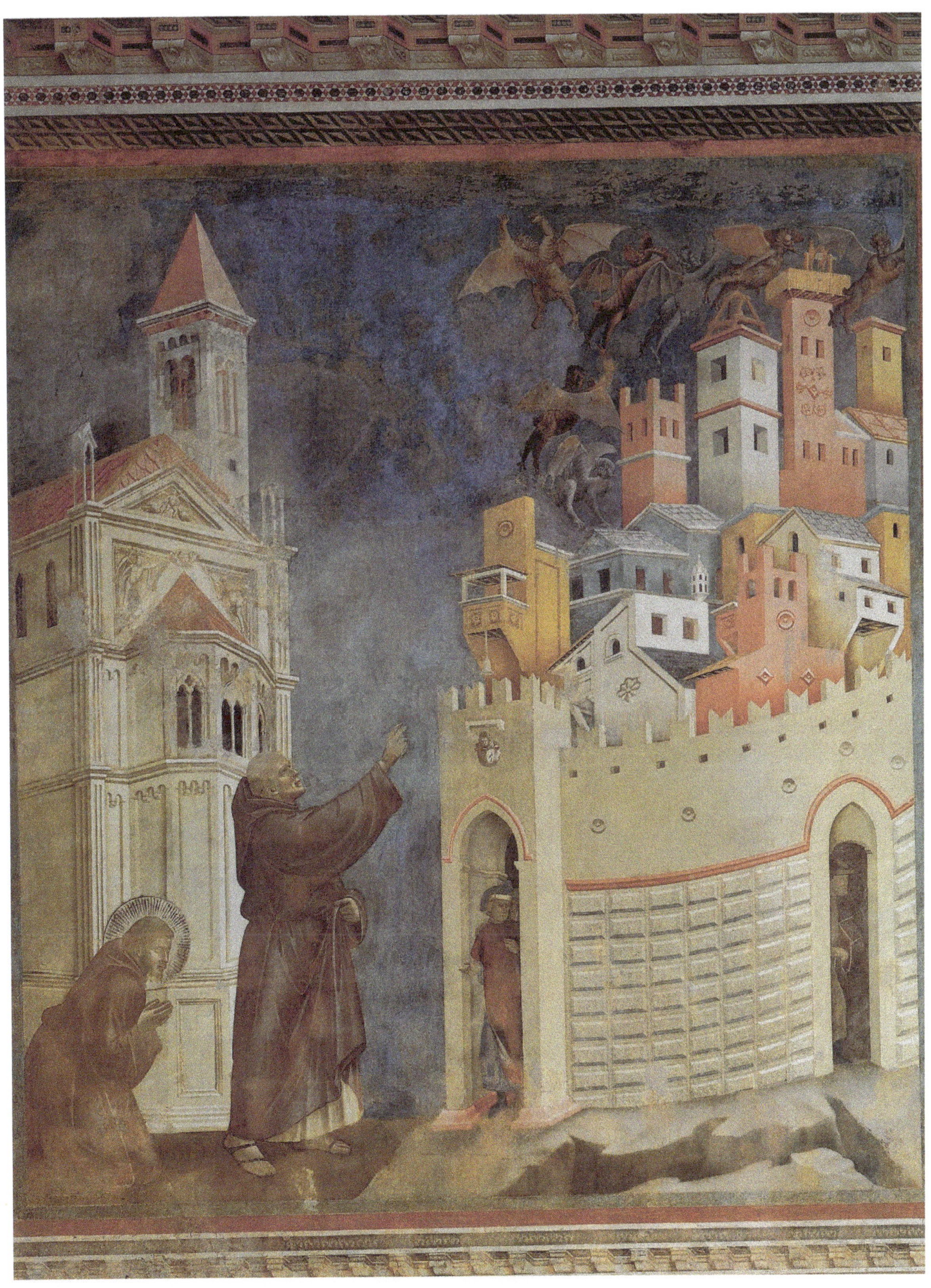

The only picture in the Louvre attributed to him, a life-size St. Francis, bears his signature yet has been of contested origins. There are two pictures in the "Galleria degli Uffizi" in Florence: the *Ognissanti Madonna* and another *Madonna* with graceful angels. In the "Galleria dell'Accademia" of the same city, are many small pictures, about a foot in height, which formerly decorated the presses or wardrobes in the sacristy of Santa Croce, representing subjects from the life and acts of Christ and St. Francis. Many that were once kept in the gallery have now been returned to their original locations. One of his finest pictures, a *Lamentation*, can be found at the Arena Chapel in Padua.

Giotto's personal character and disposition played no small part in the revolution he effected. In the union of endowments which seldom meet together in the same individual — extraordinarily inventive and poetical genius with sound, practical, energetic sense, and untiring activity and energy — Giotto resembled Rubens, and only this rare combination could have enabled him to so completely discard all the fetters of the old style, and to have executed the amazing number of works which are with reason attributed to him. His character was as independent in other matters as in his own art. There is extant a poem by Giotto, entitled *A Song against Poverty*, which becomes still more piquant in itself, and expressive of the peculiar turn of Giotto's mind, when we remember that he painted the *Glorification of Poverty* as the Bride of St. Francis and that in those days, songs in praise of poverty were as fashionable as devotion to St. Francis, the "Patriarch of poverty". Giotto was celebrated, too, for his light-hearted temperament,

his witty and satirical repartees, and he seems to have been as careful of his worldly goods as he was diligent in acquiring them.

When Giotto died, in 1336, his friend Dante had been dead three years; Petrarch was 32, and Boccaccio 23-years-old. When Petrarch died, in 1374, he left his friend Francesco da Carrara, Lord of Padua, a *Madonna* painted by Giotto, as a most precious legacy, "a wonderful piece of work, of which the ignorant might overlook the beauties, but which the learned must regard with amazement."

Visitors to Florence can look up to the Campanile with a feeling of wonder and delight, contemplating who the man must have been that conceived and executed a work so noble and supremely elegant; while, to the philosophic observer, Giotto appears as one of those few intuitively endowed beings whose development springs from a source within — one of those unconscious instruments in the hand of destiny, who, in seeking their own profit and delight through the expansion of their own faculties, make unawares a step forward in human culture, lend a new impulse to human aspirations, and, just like the "bright morning star, day's harbinger", may be submerged in the succeeding radiance, but never forgotten.

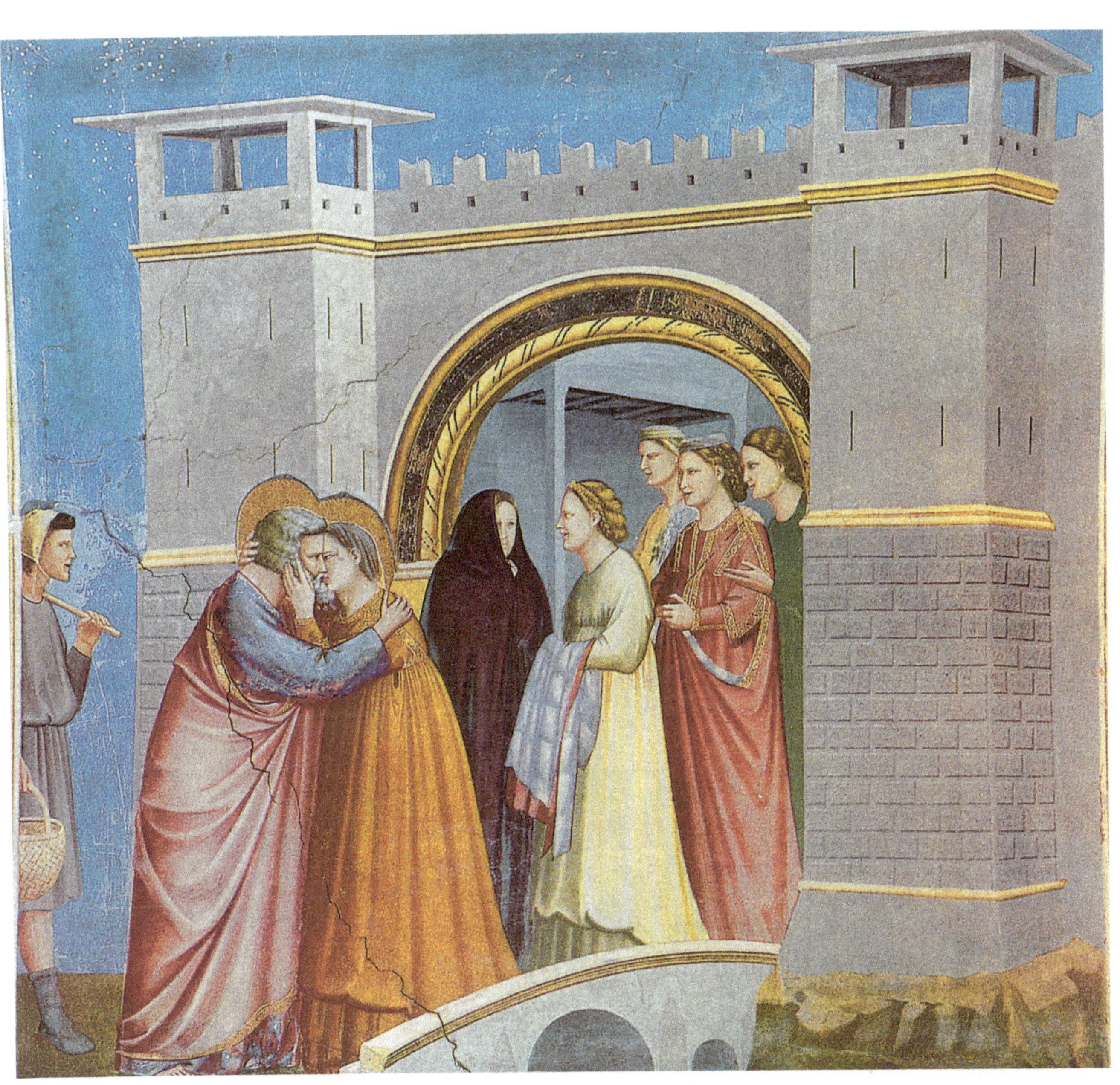

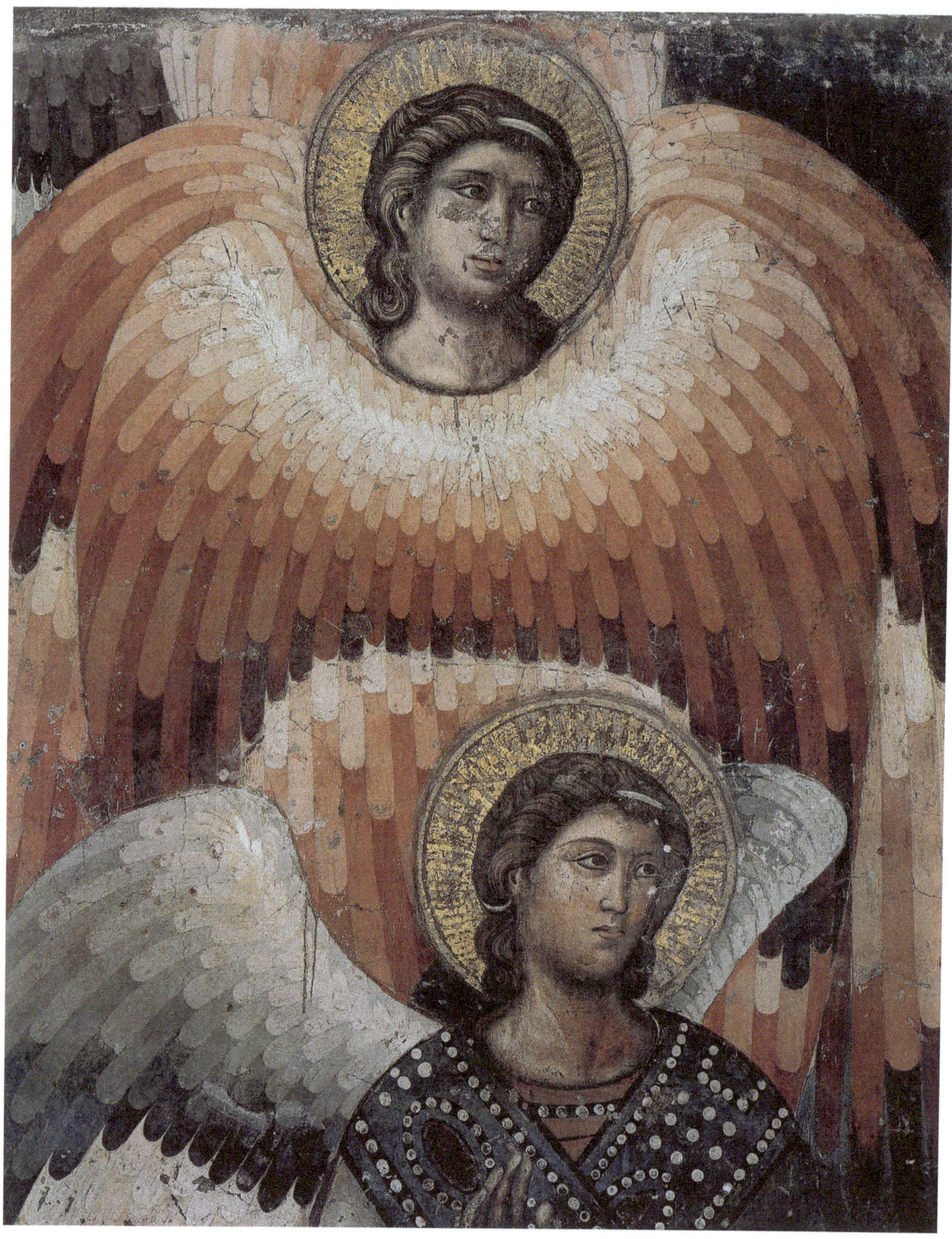

PIETRO CAVALLINI

1259-C. 1330

The birth of Pietro Cavallini has not been recorded. Born in Rome, he was an artist of the earliest epoch of the modern Roman school, and was taught painting and mosaic by Giotto while employed at Rome. In 1308 Cavallini was employed at a good salary by King Robert of Naples. Unfortunately, his works in Southern Italy have perished, but we may still assign to him a mosaic in San Crisogono in Rome, representing, on a large scale, the Virgin enthroned with the infant Christ in benediction, supported by St. James holding a book, and St. Chrysogonus, in a warrior's dress, grasping a sword. The Virgin, of a majestic presence, still displays feeble lower parts and an over proportional head. Her eyes are somewhat large and open.

Above a door, to the right inside the entrance, is a half figure of the Virgin with the infant Christ holding an orb and giving a blessing. This group is of less intricacy than the mosaics in design, and whilst the large head, slender neck, and defective hands of the Virgin betray a certain feebleness, the marked outlines, angular draperies, and absence of relief by shadow prove that Cavallini was more skilled in mosaics than in painting. Another Virgin with a puny Christ in her arms, a little less defective than the foregoing, but much repainted in the draperies, may be noticed near the chief portal. In the porch outside are two frescoes, one of which represents the *Annunciation* with a figure of a prophet, the second depicts the same subject, with the addition of God sending the infant Christ bearing a cross to the Virgin.

Cavallini, here, is a follower of the Roman school, and an eminent master. It must have been fortunate for Giotto that, on his arrival, he should have found such a man ready to assist him. After taking instruction in Rome he adopted, at least in mosaics, something of the Florentine manner. But he went still further, and in adorning the arches of San Paolo-fuori-le-Mura, he was content to carry out the designs of Giotto even after Giotto left Rome.

A spectacular *Annunciation* at the Santissima Annunziata in the Servi of Florence is a repetition, as regards the subject, of the fresco of San Marco. Richardson notes this particularity that the Virgin swoons away at the apparition of the angel. He died in 1344, at the age of eighty-five, in the odor of sanctity, having in his later years been a man of eminent piety. The only disciple of Cavallini is Giovanni da Pistoia.

◀ **Pietro Cavallini,**
Seraphims, c. 1293.
Fresco.
Santa Cecilia in Trastevere, Rome.

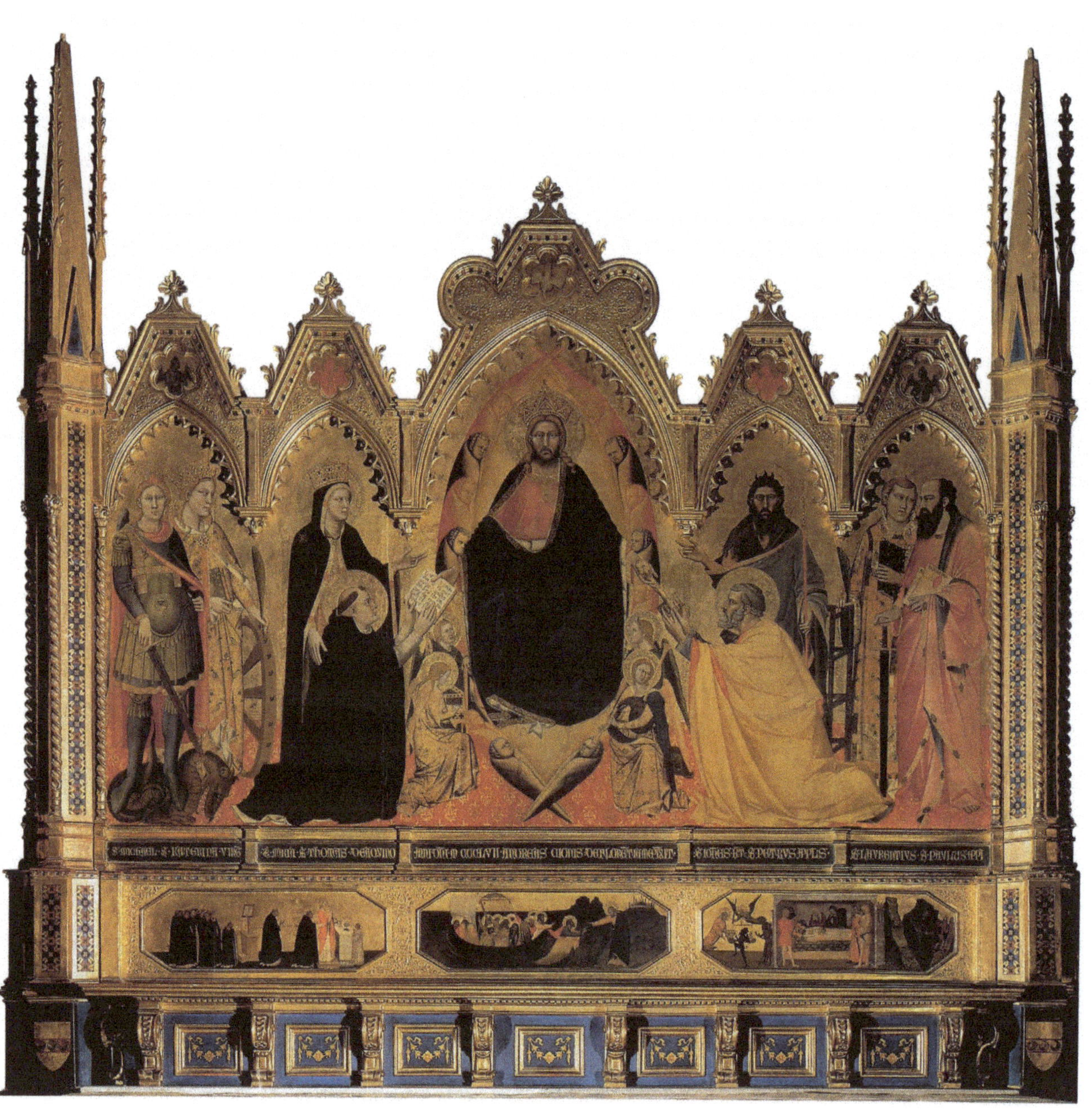

ANDREA ORCAGNA

c. 1308-1368

Andrea Orcagna was the son of a goldsmith in Florence. The goldsmiths of the fourteenth and fifteenth centuries were generally excellent designers and frequently became painters. Andrea Orcagna apparently learned design under the tuition of his father. The dates of Orcagna's birth and death are not exactly known, but Rosini places his birth prior to 1310, because by 1332 he had already acquired so much celebrity that he was called upon to continue the decoration of the Campo Santo at Pisa. Andrea Orcagna selected subjects which harmonized with these sacred precincts, they were to represent in four great compartments: Death, Judgment, Hell or Purgatory, and Paradise; but only three were completed.

The first is styled the *Triumph of Death*. It is full of poetry and abounding in ideas then new in pictorial art. On the right is a festive company of ladies and cavaliers, who, according to their falcons and dogs, appear to have returned from a hunt. They are seated, splendidly attired, under orange trees with rich carpets spread at their feet.

◀ **Andrea Orcagna,**
Strozzi Altarpiece, 1354-1357.
Tempera on wood, 160 x 296 cm.
Santa Maria Novella, Florence.

A troubadour amuses them with flattering songs. All the pleasures of sense and joys of earth are united here. On the left Death approaches with rapid flight — a fearful-looking woman with wild streaming hair, claws instead of nails, large bat wings, and indestructible wire-woven drapery. She swings a scythe in her hand, and is on the point of mowing down the joys of the company.

A host of corpses closely pressed together lie at her feet; based on their insignia they are almost all recognized as the former rulers of the world: kings, queens, cardinals, bishops, princes, warriors, etc. Their souls rise out of them in the form of newborn infants as angels and demons prepare to receive them; the souls of the pious fold their hands in prayer, while those of the condemned shrink back in horror. The angels are peculiarly yet happily conceived with bird-like forms and variegated plumage; the demons have the semblance of beasts of prey or of disgusting reptiles and fight amongst themselves. Next to these corpses is a crowd of beggars and cripples, who call upon Death to end their sorrows with outstretched arms. Traditionally, among the personages in these pictures are many portraits of the artist's contemporaries.

The second representation is the *Last Judgment*. Above, in the centre, Christ and the Virgin are

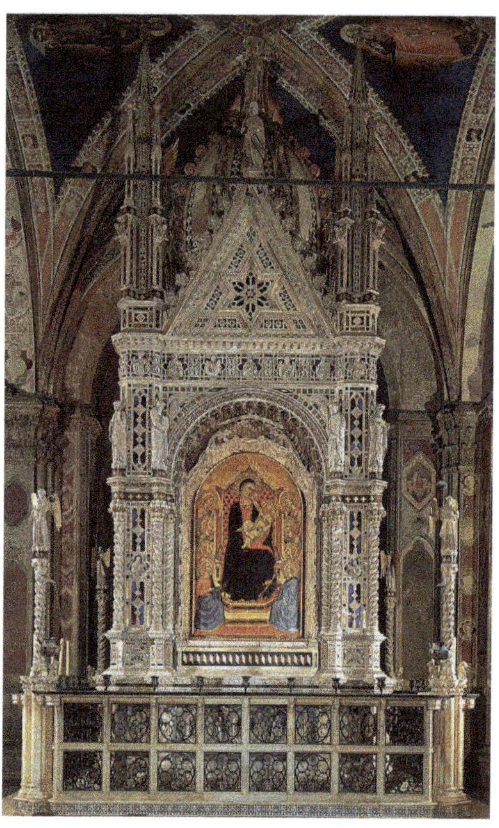

who, while rising, seems doubtful to which side he should turn; here a hypocritical monk, whom an angel draws back by the hair from the path to heaven; and a youth in a lively and rich costume, whom another angel leads away to Paradise. The attitudes of Christ and the Virgin were later borrowed by Michelangelo in his celebrated *Last Judgment*; but, notwithstanding the perfection of his forms, he stands below the dignified grandeur of the old master. Later painters also borrowed from his arrangement of the patriarchs and apostles — particularly Fra Bartolomeo and Raphael.

The third representation, directly succeeding the foregoing, is *Hell*. It is said to have been executed from Andrea's design by his brother Bernardo. Hell is represented as a great rocky caldron, divided into four compartments rising one above the other. In the midst sits Satan, a fearful armed giant, himself a fiery furnace whose body emits flames to different places and in which sinners are consumed or crushed. In other parts the condemned are seen spitted like fowls, roasted and basted by demons, with other scenes of atrocities too horrible and sickening for description. The lower part of the picture was crudely painted over and altered according to the taste of the sixteenth century.

enthroned in separate glories. He turns to the left, towards the condemned, while he uncovers the wound in his side, and raises his right arm with a menacing gesture, his countenance full of majestic wrath. The Virgin, on the right of her son, is the picture of heavenly mercy as she appealingly looks toward Christ, pressing her hand to the bosom which nourished him in a plea for sinners. On either side are arranged the prophets of the Old Testament, the apostles, and other saints — severe, solemn, dignified figures. Angels, holding the instruments of the *Passion*, hover over Christ and the Virgin; under them is a group of archangels. Lower down is the earth, where men are seen rising from their graves; armed angels directing them to the right and left. Here, King Solomon,

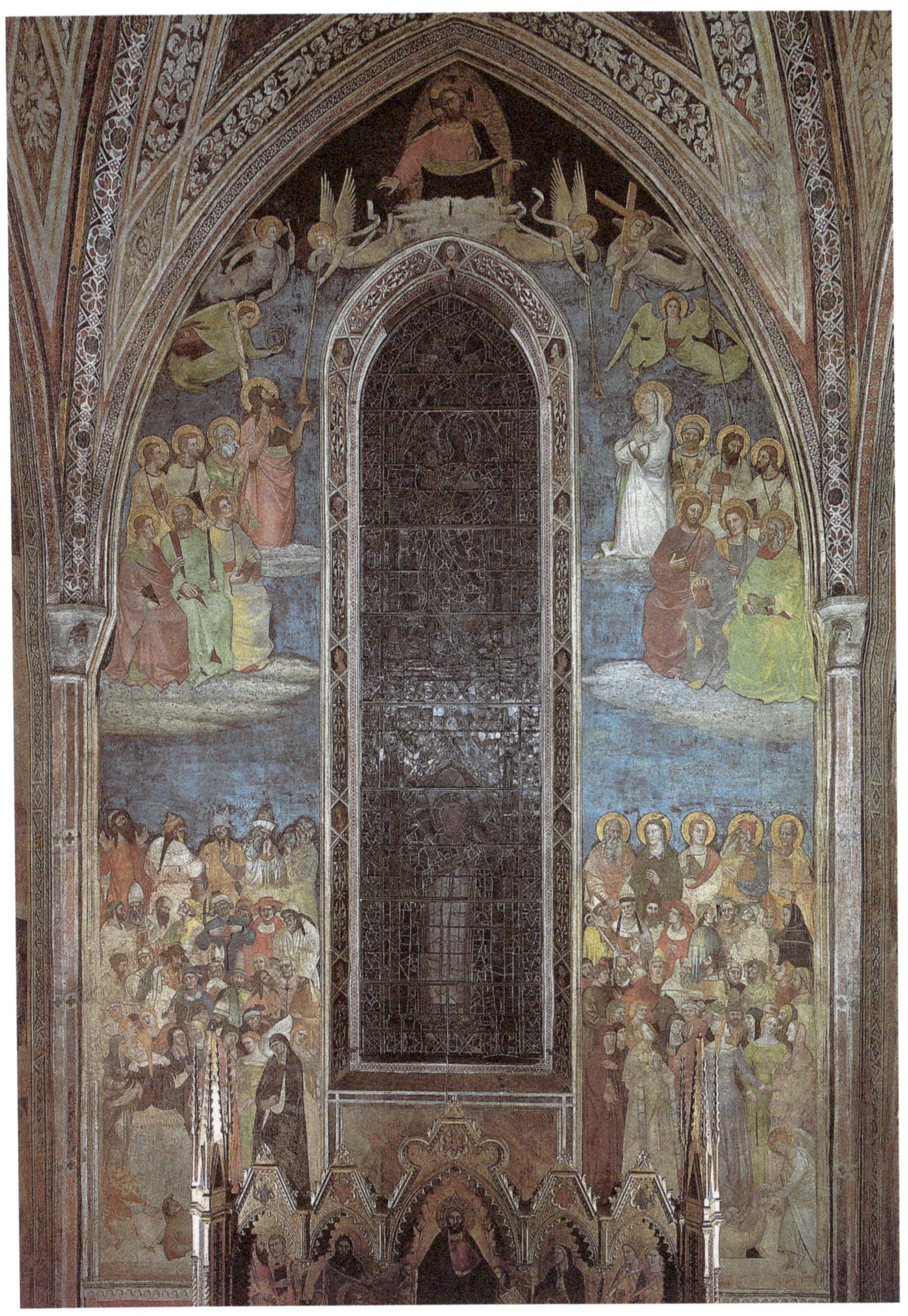

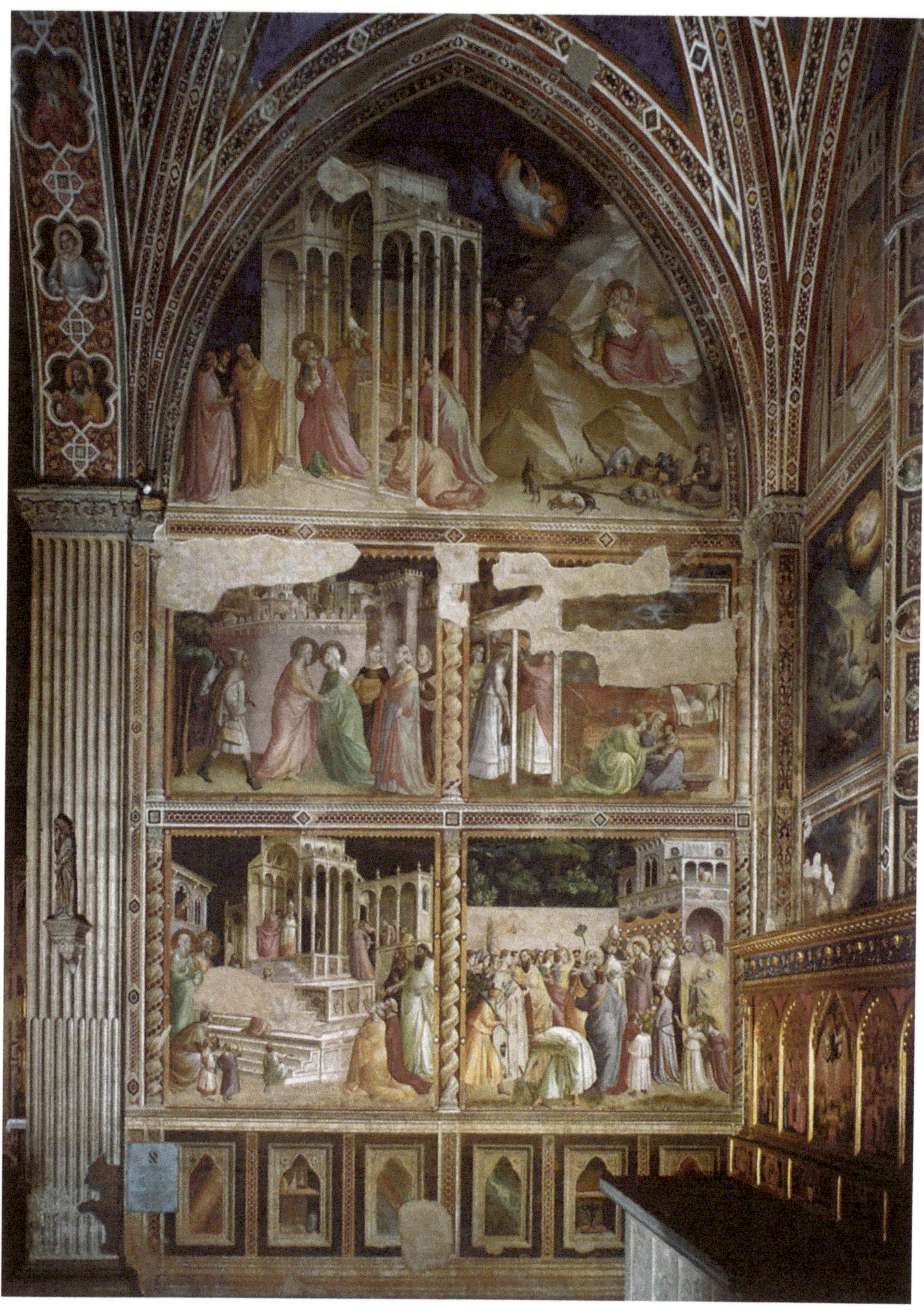

TADDEO GADDI

c. 1300-1366

W e should now return to the pupils of Giotto. Taddeo Gaddi; he was Giotto's favorite scholar, as well as his godson. His pictures are considered to be the most important works of the fourteenth century. They resemble the manner of Giotto in the feeling for truth, nature, and simplicity; however, we also find improved execution in them, exhibiting even more beauty, largeness, and grandeur of style.

His pictures are numerous, several are in the Galleria dell'Accademia in Florence and the Gemäldegalerie in Berlin, one can be seen in the Metropolitan Museum of Modern Art in New York. In the National Gallery in London, are two large panels which probably formed the two wings of a central piece (an "Enthroned Madonna," or a "Coronation of the Virgin"), filled with figures of saints who appear to be in attendance of some grand ceremony or important personage, all the heads are finely distinguished in character.

◀ **Taddeo Gaddi,**
Scenes from the Life of the Virgin, 1328-1330.
Fresco.
Baroncelli Chapel, Basilica di Santa Croce, Florence.

▲ **Taddeo Gaddi,**
Saint Eligius in the Goldsmith's Shop, c. 1365.
Tempera on panel, 35 x 39 cm.
Museo del Prado, Madrid.

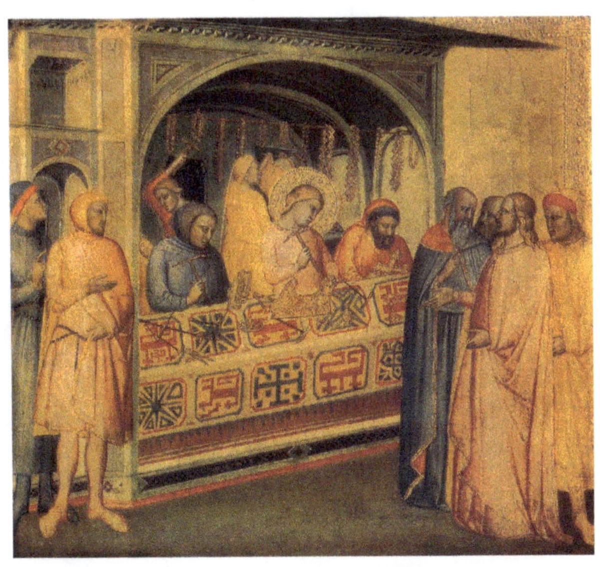

There are four small pictures which he painted to be found in the Louvre, and four grander ones in the Gemäldegalerie in Berlin. Between Taddeo Gaddi and Simone Martini there existed an ardent friendship and a mutual admiration, which did honor to both. He was, like many of the old painters, a skilful architect and built the *Ponte Vecchio* (Old Bridge) in Florence, which is still standing and famous for the goldsmiths' shops which line it on either side. After Giotto, there was no name more celebrated in his time than that of Taddeo Gaddi.

Gaddi died in 1366, leaving behind two sons, Agnolo and Giovanni, who were also both painters.

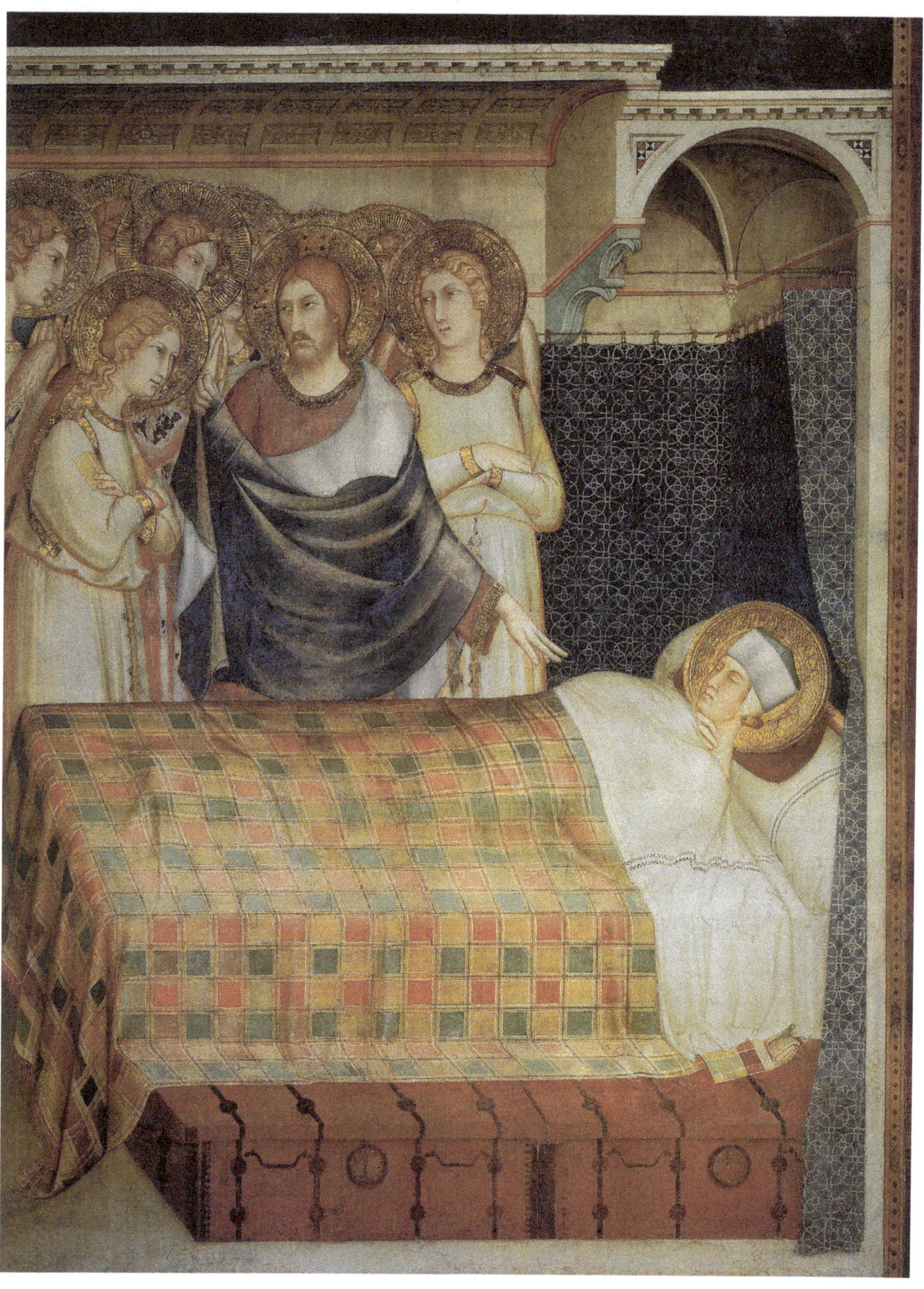

SIMONE MARTINI, ALSO CALLED SIMONE MEMMI

c. 1284-1344

Simone Martini, commonly, but not correctly called Simone Memmi, was born in 1283. He followed the manner of painting proper to his native Siena, as improved by Duccio, which is essentially different from the style of Giotto and his school, and the idea that Simone was himself a pupil of Giotto is therefore wide of the mark. The Sienese style is less natural, dignified and reserved than the Florentine; it has less unity of impression, has more tendencies to pietism, and is marked by exaggerations which are partly related to the obsolescent Byzantine manner, and partly seem to forebode certain peculiarities of the fully developed art which we find prevalent in Michelangelo. Simone, in especial, tended to an excessive and rather affected tenderness in his female figures; he was more successful in single figures and in portraits than in large compositions of incident. He finishes with scrupulous minuteness, and was elaborate in decorations, patterning and gilding.

◀ **Simone Martini,**
The Dream of St. Martin, c. 1317.
Fresco, 65 x 200 cm.
Lower Basilica of San Francesco, Assisi.

The first known fresco of Simone is the vast one which he executed in the hall of the Palazzo Pubblico in Siena – the *Madonna Enthroned with the Infant*, and a number of angels and saints; its date is 1315, at which period he was already an artist of repute throughout Italy. In S. Lorenzo Maggiore of Naples he painted a life-sized picture of King Robert, crowned by his brother Lewis, bishop of Toulouse; this is also extant, but much damaged. In 1320 he painted for the high altar of the church of S. Catarina in Pisa the *Virgin and Child between six saints*; above are archangels, apostles and other figures. The compartmented portions of the work are now dispersed, some of them being in the academy of Siena. Towards 1321 he executed for the church of S. Domenico in Orvieto a picture of the bishop of Savona kneeling before the Madonna attended by saints, now in the Fabriceria of the cathedral. Certain frescoes in Assisi in the chapel of San Martino, representing the life of that saint, ascribed by Vasari to Puccio Capanne, are now, upon evidence, assigned to Simone. He also painted, in the south transept of the lower church of the same edifice, figures of the Virgin and eight saints. In 1328 he produced for the sala del consilio in Siena a striking equestrian portrait of the victorious general Guidoriccio Fogliani de Ricci.

Simone conceived the infant Christ plump and round-cheeked, with a pouting lip, vast forehead, short curly locks, and a glance more threatening than kind. He clothed him in a rich dress, and thus brought the art to a point where it seems to claim admiration more by richness and abundance of ornament than by simplicity or beauty of shape and features. The graceful female saints reveal the tendency common to Duccio and Simone, to contrast the stern gravity of males with an excessive tenderness in the other sex. A careful execution marks every portion of the work, whose color can hardly be criticized. The composition, too, has the defects of Duccio and is distributed without the perfect balance of the Florentines. It betrays a wish, or the necessity under which the artist labored, of preserving old forms of arrangement, dictated no doubt by custom.

Simone had married in 1324 Giovanna, the daughter of Memmo (Guglielmo) di Fillipuccio. Her brother named Lippo Memmi, was also a painter, and was frequently associated with Simone in his work; and this is the only reason why Simone has come down to us with the family-name Memmi. They painted together in 1333 the *Annunciation* which is now in the Uffizi gallery. Simone kept a bottega (or shop) undertaking any ornamental work, and his gains were large. In 1339 he settled at the papal court in Avignon, where he made the acquaintance

of Petrarch and Laura, and he painted for the poet a portrait of his lady, which gave occasion for two of Petrarch's sonnets, in which Simone is eulogized. He also illuminated for the poet a copy of the commentary of Servius upon Virgil, now preserved in the Ambrosian library of Milan.

He was largely employed in the decorations of the papal buildings in Avignon, and several of his works still remain in the cathedral, in the hall of the consistory, and, in the two chapels of the palace, the stories of the stories of the Baptist, and of Stephen and other saints. One of the latest productions (1342) is the picture of *Christ found by his parents in the Temple*, now in the Liverpool gallery. Simone died in Avignon in 1344. Simone was certainly one of the most remarkable and interesting painters of his time, and quite independent of the influence of Giotto.

Simone Martini, ▶
The Annunciation, 1333.
Tempera on panel, 184 x 210 cm.
Galleria degli Uffizi, Florence.

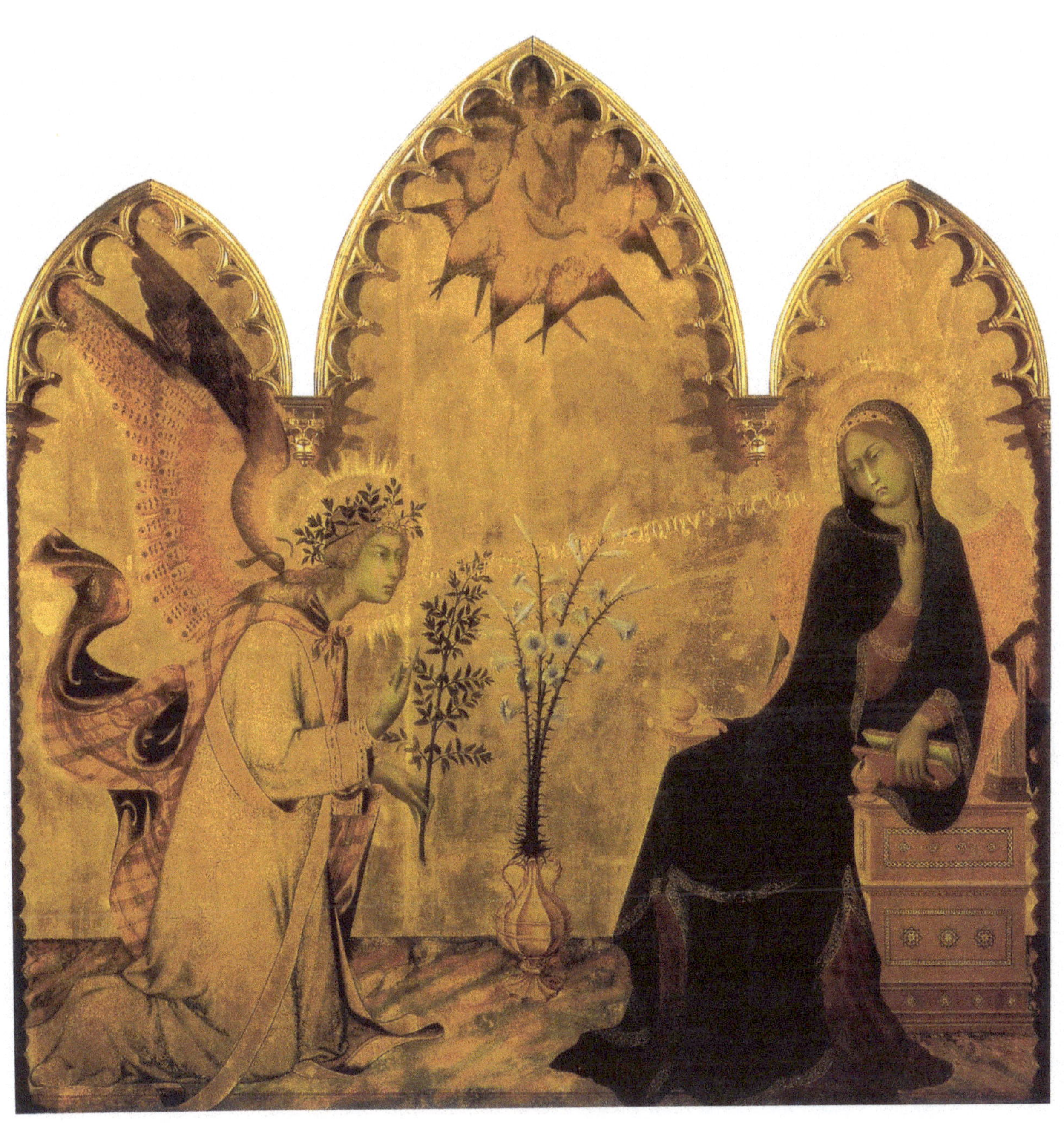

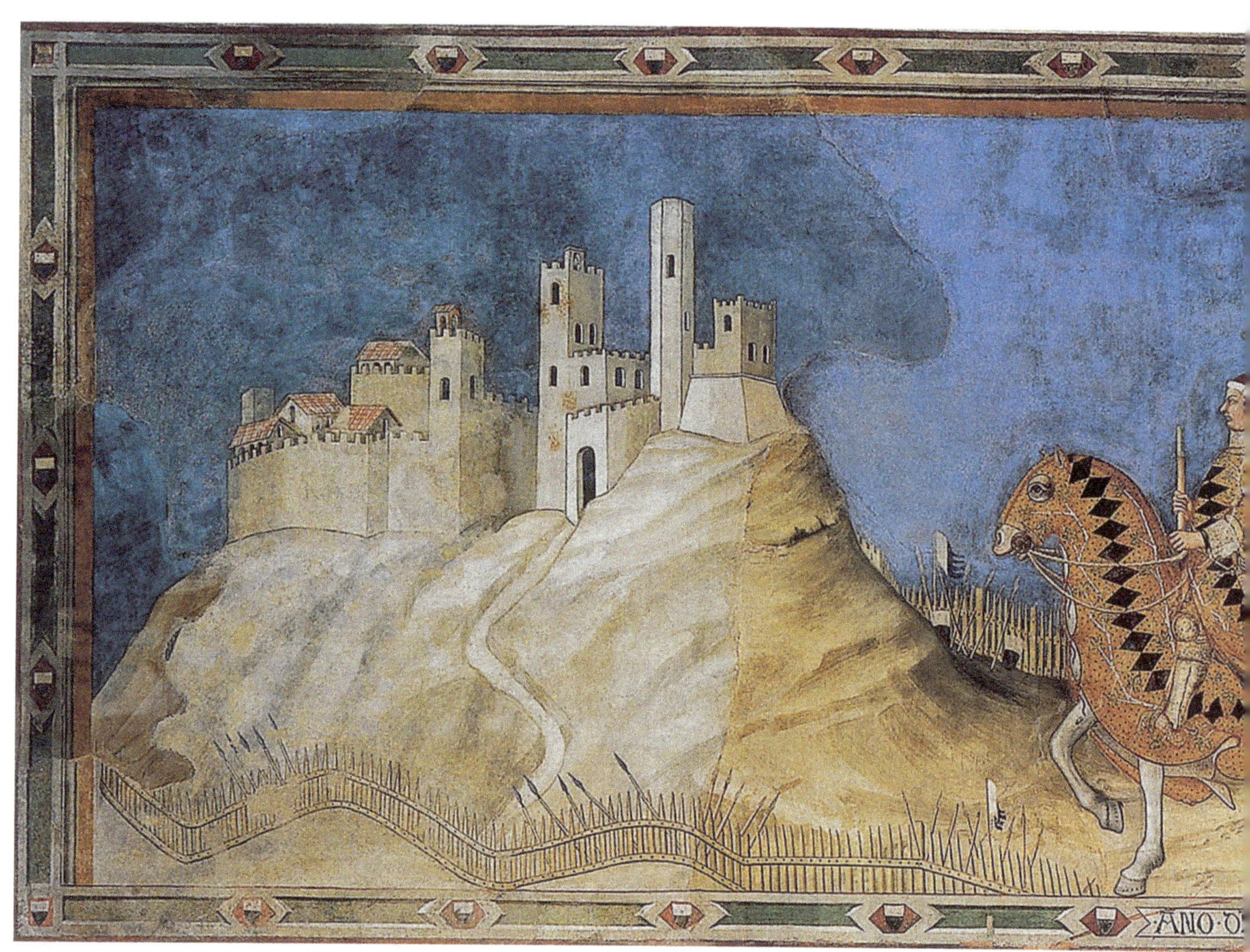

▲ **Simone Martini**,
Guidoriccio da Fogliano, c. 1328.
Fresco, 340 x 968 cm.
Palazzo Pubblico, Siena.

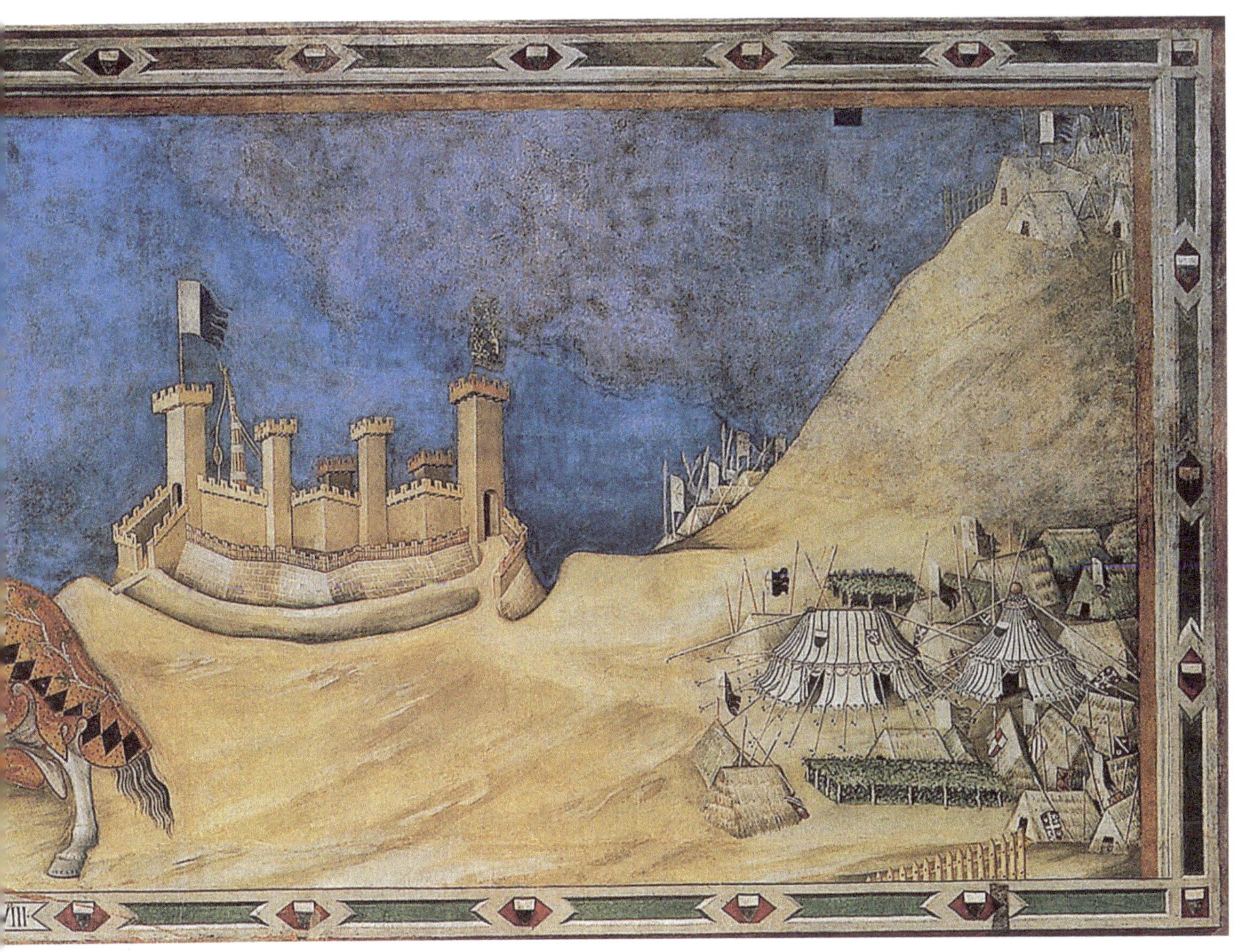

LIST OF ILLUSTRATIONS

ART HISTORY COLLECTION

Abstract Art

Art Deco

Art Nouveau

Baroque

Byzantine Art

Chinese Art

Cubism

Dada

Early Italian Art

Egypt Art

Expressionism

Gothic Art

Greek Art

Impressionism

Indian Art

Naive Art

Neoclassicism

Persian Art

Post-Impressionism

Realism

Renaissance

Pre-Raphaelites

Rococo

Roman Art

Romanesque Art

Romanticism

Surrealism

Symbolism

The Fauves

The Viennese Secession